PERGAMON INTERNATIONAL LIBRARY
of Science, Technology, Engineering and Social Studies
The 1000-volume original paperback library in aid of education,
industrial training and the enjoyment of leisure
Publisher : Robert Maxwell, M.C.

ADULT EDUCATION IN DEVELOPING COUNTRIES

THE PERGAMON TEXTBOOK INSPECTION COPY SERVICE

An inspection copy of any book published in the Pergamon International Library will gladly be sent to academic staff without obligation for their consideration for course adoption or recommendation. Copies may be retained for a period of 60 days from receipt and returned if not suitable. When a particular title is adopted or recommended for adoption for class use and the recommendation results in a sale of 12 or more copies, the inspection copy may be retained with our compliments. The Publishers will be pleased to receive suggestions for revised editions and new titles to be published in this important International Library.

Titles of Interest

M. L. BATAILLE:
A Turning Point for Literacy

M. BLAUG:
Economics of Education: A Selected Annotated Bibliography

D. F. BRATCHELL:
The Aims and Organization of Further Education

R. H. DAVE:
Foundations of Lifelong Education

J. L. HENDERSON:
Education for World Understanding

F. W. JESSUP:
Lifelong Learning: A Symposium on Continuing Education

P. RITTER:
Educreation: A Milestone in Educational Thought for an Evolving Society

J. THRETHEWAY:
Comparative Education

ADULT EDUCATION IN DEVELOPING COUNTRIES

Second edition

BY

EDWIN K. TOWNSEND COLES

PERGAMON PRESS
OXFORD · NEW YORK · TORONTO
SYDNEY · PARIS · FRANKFURT

U.K.	Pergamon Press Ltd., Headington Hill Hall, Oxford OX3 0BW, England
U.S.A.	Pergamon Press Inc., Maxwell House, Fairview Park, Elmsford, New York 10523, U.S.A.
CANADA	Pergamon of Canada Ltd., 75 The East Mall, Toronto, Ontario, Canada
AUSTRALIA	Pergamon Press (Aust.) Pty. Ltd., 19a Boundary Street, Rushcutters Bay, N.S.W. 2011, Australia
FRANCE	Pergamon Press SARL, 24 rue des Ecoles, 75240 Paris, Cedex 05, France
WEST GERMANY	Pergamon Press GmbH, 6242 Kronberg-Taunus, Pferdstrasse 1, West Germany

First edition 1969

Second edition 1977

Library of Congress Cataloging in Publication Data

Townsend Coles, Edwin Keith.
Adult education in developing countries.

Includes bibliographical references and index.
1. Adult education—Africa, Central. I. Title.
LC5258.C4T6 1976   374.9'67   76-27713
ISBN 0-08-021293-X (hard cover)

Printed in Great Britain by A. Wheaton & Co., Exeter

For
Susan,
Caroline and
Miranda

Contents

List of Diagrams and Tables

Preface

The first edition of this book was written nearly 10 years ago. At that time I had just returned to the United Kingdom after 8 years in what was then known as "Central Africa"—Malawi, Southern Rhodesia and Zambia—and I wished to record the developments I had noticed in adult education both there and in other third world countries. At that time adult education was still regarded as something of a peripheral activity—good, but not essential—and in the context of Southern Rhodesia a dangerous commodity to be handled with caution.

Since then much has happened. In 10 years adult education has at last received the verbal recognition it deserves as an indispensible part of education in any country, whether developing or so-called developed. Unesco has held its third, and what really was the fourth, international conference[1] on adult education at Tokyo in 1972. An International Council on Adult Education has been established under the distinguished patronage of the President of the United Republic of Tanzania, with Professor J. R. Kidd, an internationally respected professor of adult education, as its Secretary-General. A follow-up meeting to the 1965 Teheran Conference on Illiteracy was held at Persepolis in 1975. And in addition to these international events there have been countless regional, national and local developments which indicate the rising prestige of adult education. At last it has come of age, and no longer has to go apologetically, cap in hand, seeking recognition.

It was time that the changed situation was reflected by a second edition of a book which was still widely being used in universities and teaching colleges as a basic text.

Not that there is not a growing literature on adult education. Much

---

[1]The first international conference on adult education was held in Cambridge in 1929, sponsored by the World Association of Adult Education, an organization which shortly afterwards became one of the casualties of the disturbed 1930s.

is now available. There is, however, a continuing need for a book which outlines in general terms the how?, what? and who? of adult education as applied to the third world, and this is what this volume seeks to do. It is written primarily for those either pursuing training or who are in some branch of educational administration, statutory or non-statutory, and who need to have answers to these fundamental questions. Rather than attempting to push the frontiers of knowledge back, it seeks to consolidate what has already been achieved; to translate the theory of the innovators into practical and attainable goals.

A reviewer of the first edition took me to task for having attempted to write a comprehensive book on adult education in developing countries. Writing from the safe confines of a provincial British university he argued that each country must be treated individually. Of course, he is right, and had I neglected this fact I should have deserved wholesale condemnation. Each country must be treated as a special case. Nevertheless, I have now worked in or paid official visits to over twenty developing countries, admittedly mostly in Africa, and whilst I am aware of the differences and the need to regard each and every one as being a unique combination of circumstances, I am also struck by the similarities—by the way in which somewhat similar situations and problems do, in fact, recur time and time again. It is for this reason that I have ventured to use the same title for the second edition as the first. In my view it is possible in general but still useful terms to write about the theory and practice of adult education in developing countries.

Acknowledgements

Whilst taking full responsibility for everything written in this book, I cannot fail to recognize my enormous indebtedness to many people who in various ways have contributed to my better understanding of the subject and consequently contributed in some measure to this present volume.

I am especially grateful to Paul Bertelsen, Chief of the Adult Education Section at Unesco, for having read earlier drafts and made valuable comments. I am also indebted to John Lowe of the Organization for Economic Co-operation and Development, Paris, and to Hanuš Körner, a colleague in Unesco, for their advice. Werner Keweloh of the German Adult Education Association and now Director of its Africa Bureau has been a constant source of ideas and information.

In my work for Unesco and the International Bank for Reconstruction and Development I have been fortunate to have come into contact with adult educationists in many countries; I have cause to think especially of Roby Kidd in Canada, Josef Müller of the Federal Republic of Germany, Kwasi Ampene of Ghana, Peter Kechayopoulos with whom I worked for two years in Greece, Asher Deleon, the Unesco Adviser on adult education in India, Al Aimé in Lesotho and John Bolton-Maggs in Liberia, Mike Seeyave on Mauritius, and Lalage Bown and Akunde Tugbyele in Nigeria.

There are also the very many men, women and youths I have met taking part in adult educational activities as learners, teachers, leaders and administrators from whom I have gained a better insight into what adult education really means in the lives of individual people. To them, too, I wish to record my thanks.

The task of deciphering my handwriting and preparing the manuscript has been undertaken by my friend Valerie Saunders with efficiency, patience and humour; my warm thanks go to her.

Paris   E.K.T.C.

Prologue[1]

Principle
The normal culmination of the educational process is adult education.

Considerata
There are many possible definitions of adult education. For a very large number of adults in the world today, it is a substitute for the basic education they missed. For the many individuals who received only a very incomplete education, it is the complement to elementary or professional education. For those whom it helps respond to new demands which their environment makes on them, it is the prolongation of education. It offers further education to those who have already received high-level training. And it is a means of individual development for everybody. One or other of these aspects may be more important in one country than in another, but they all have their validity. Adult education can no longer be limited to rudimentary levels, or confined to "cultural" education for a minority.

Adult education assumes especial importance to the extent that it may be decisive in the success of non-adults' school activities. For children's primary education—a primordial objective—cannot be dissociated from their parents' educational levels. The rising generations cannot be properly trained in an illiterate environment. Since the development of education depends on using to the full the capacities of all people able to teach or help train others, the number of professional people engaged in working towards educational objectives can only be increased by intensifying adult education. We should never

---

[1]*Learning to Be: the world of education today and tomorrow:* The Fauré Report, Unesco, Paris, 1972, pp. 205-206. Copyright, Unesco 1972. Reprinted by permission of Unesco.

set adult education against the education of children and young people: the concept of global or over-all education goes beyond the semblance of contradiction, enabling the two extremes to be enlisted, parallel to each other and at the same time, in the service of common educational objectives, in the broadest sense.

It follows that adult education can no longer be a fringe sector of activity in any society and must be given its own proper place in educational policies and budgets. This means that school and out-of-school education must be linked firmly together.

Recommendation

Educational strategies in the coming decade should have rapid development of adult education, in school and out of school, as one of their priority objectives.

Comment

Given the fact that present facilities are lagging far behind the world adult population's educational and cultural needs, step-by-step progress is not enough: what is required is a giant leap forward. This can only be achieved if private individuals and public bodies join in contributing both effort and resources. Action must be taken to:

Utilize all existing scholastic establishments (primary, secondary, technical schools) for adult-education activities, and to increase the number of adults admitted to higher education institutions.

Create special adult-education institutions or integrate out-of-school activities, to assist adults to function better as citizens, producers, consumers and parents.

Promote the organization of individual and community educational activities, encourage self-education, develop spontaneous initiative and make all educational means available to the greatest number.

This three-point action can only be carried out with financial and technical support from state and government and co-operation from both the industrial and agricultural sectors of the economy. But much of the work to be done depends on individual and group initiative. This role of private initiative provides an essential guarantee that both freedom and diversity will be respected, and encourages pedagogic innovation.

CHAPTER 1

Aims and Purposes

The 1960s and 1970s will be remembered as a time of ferment in education. There is not a branch of the profession which has not been affected by the strong wind of change which has been blowing throughout the world. Whereas formerly changes in education were seen more in the light of slight adaptations to existing structures and practices, the past two decades have witnessed insistent demands for wholesale renovation of systems in order that they may better fulfil their tasks in the contemporary world. Education is to be something relevant to the whole of life, contributing to the material, social and cultural improvement of each individual from childhood to old age. If one characteristic of this period is to be selected as the most significant it is surely the return to the concept, known and practiced in former times, of lifelong education; that the whole of life is a learning experience and that those responsible for education should construct their plans within this overall guiding principle.

Crisis in the Third World

The crisis in education which has been so marked a feature of this period has not been confined to the so-called developed countries. It has manifested itself with equal vigour in the developing countries where, as they became independent, each sought to examine their inherited educational systems and to make adaptations to bring them more in line with contemporary needs. Generally the solution which was initially favoured was to expand whatever was there; thus a main aim in most countries was to adopt plans leading to a full primary course of 6 or 7 years' schooling for all children. As to renovation and overhaul, in the early stages comparatively little was done, and

1

the form and content of the inherited systems were subject only to slight modification. International aid was most readily available in the conventional areas of education and rapid expansion thus took place in primary, secondary and tertiary institutions.

Emergence of Adult and Non-formal Education

A negative attitude which the developing countries had inherited from the former colonial powers was a scant regard for any form of education which fell outside of the normal pyramid of formal advancement from school to university. This was not done with malice aforethought but simply a reflection of prevailing attitudes to any education not directed towards children and youths. Adult education had been established in the developed countries largely by non-governmental agencies and it was principally to them that the task fell in the developing countries. It was not until the 1950s, when adult education was beginning to be recognized as a discrete and serious branch of education in Europe and North America, that some note was being taken of the contribution which it could make to the development of third world countries. This was the period when fundamental education programmes became the vogue in developing countries, soon to be superseded by the more dynamic concept of community development, with both of which literacy was associated. But financial allocations to adult education were meagre, and it was not until quite recently that fresh assessments were made of the potential role which it should play in development.

The reasons which imposed countries to think again about the form and content of the educational provision they were making are not hard to find. The spiralling costs of formal education have placed an intolerable burden which countries increasingly find difficult to sustain. The automatic assumption that school provision must increase from year to year has had to be questioned. Rising populations have demanded accelerated school building programmes; all but a few countries, however, have been unable to keep pace with the new claimants for places. Each year there may be more children in school, but each year also there are more children uncatered for.[1] Such a situation clearly calls for fresh thinking; whether the continuing provision of more places in schools as conventionally conceived is both wise and within the financial competence of a country, or whether some other form of education cannot be established which is equally effective, possibly less costly, and which reaches out to a mass audience rather than to smaller narrowly defined groups within the community; one which will also enable provision to be made for the rising number of young adults who have missed out altogether on formal schooling. For more children out of school today means more adults needing education and training tomorrow.

At the same time there is a growing concern whether the formal system, divorced as it so often is from the general life of society, should be regarded as the only proper means of education; whether for many a more flexible approach would not be preferable, re-affirming what was accepted in most traditional societies that there should be a close inter-relationship between the life of work and the life of learning. The formal system may be appropriate for some but it should not be regarded as the only ladder for advancement both on educational as well as economic grounds. That alternative ways have to be examined, such as those being successfully implemented in the Republic of China where school and work are regarded as integral parts of development. And this reassessment of education for the

---

[1]Figures for out-of-school young people in the less developed regions (LDR) of the world have been estimated as follows (in millions):

	Ages 6 - 11			Ages 12 - 17		
	1965	1975	1985	1965	1975	1985
LDR	114	128	165	150	177	240
East Asia	0.8	0.1	0.1	6	5	4
South Asia	71	80	98	98	116	162
Africa	29	34	49	31	37	50
Latin America	14	13	17	19	21	26

Although the percentage of out-of-school young people will decline from 58 per cent in 1965 to 50 per cent in 1985, the *absolute number* of children out-of-school will increase from 264 millions in 1965 to 405 million in 1985, i.e. by some 53 per cent.

From "Educational development, world and regional statistical trends and projections until 1985", a background paper for the World Population Conference, Bucharest, 1974, Unesco, 1975, p. 15.

young is taking place at the same moment as there is also the global reaffirmation that learning must be regarded as a lifelong process. That the young need to learn how to learn; and that thereafter to each and every individual should be given such opportunity as is possible to continue with their learning. Indeed it is now universally recognized that what can be learnt at school is but an introduction to life; that knowledge in every sphere is accumulating and changing so rapidly that learning must of necessity be a continuing activity. Nor is it just that new knowledge has to be learnt; every individual has also to become accommodated to a changing society in a changing world. And nowhere is this more apparent than in the countries of the third world, many of which are undergoing social revolutions as profound as the complementary changes in their economic structure. For a person to be enabled to make their fullest contribution to life, no matter what are their circumstances, mode of living or level of education, they must be given both vocational skills and the chance of understanding the society and the total environment in which they are living. Advancement has both its economic and social facets, and both must be catered for.

Adult Education and Development

There was a time when development was measured in purely economic terms. Gradually there has come the recognition "that there could be growth without development, growth in economic terms without development in the sense of improved conditions of living for the majority of the people".[2] Elaborate manpower surveys, statistical projections and cost-benefit analyses have their undoubted value, but they are not the whole picture. Development obviously has its economic side, and important it is. But people are people; if the human resources of a country are viewed in the same manner as the mineral and animal reserves a grossly distorted image will inevitably ensue. For real development must depend on the balanced growth of the person, both as an economic and a social being. Harbison has rightly argued that "the wealth of a country is dependent upon more than its

---

[2]*Learner-centred Innovations in Literacy,* by Helen Callaway, International Symposium for Literacy, Persepolis, 1975, p. 4.

natural resources and material capital; it is determined in significant degree by the knowledge, skills and motivation of its ·people".[3] It is in recognition of this that added impetus has been given to adult education, since so much that has to be comprehended and understood requires an adult mind with an adult's experience of life.

There are thus strong grounds, based both on common justice for all as well as the need for improved economic competence, for adult education to be taken seriously as a branch of education worthy of consideration equal to that accorded to the conventional formal system. Before proceeding further it is necessary to be clear what is meant by the term adult education.

Adult Education: Definition

In recent years there have been several attempts to provide a comprehensive definition of adult education which breaks down the barriers which once existed between "adult", "further", "vocational" and "technical" education. For adult education is increasingly being seen in its totality. Thus Liveright and Haygood proposed that "adult education is the process whereby persons who no longer (or did not) attend school on a regular and full-time basis undertake sequential and organized activities with a conscious intention of bringing about changes in information, knowledge, understanding or skills, appreciation and attitudes; or for the purpose of identifying and solving personal or community problems".[4]

Bertelsen has further refined the definition in order to take greater account of informal education. His definition is simply that "adult education is any learning experience designed for adults irrespective of content, level and methods used . . .".[5]

The most recent definition comes also from Unesco[6] and states that "the term adult education denotes the entire body of organized edu-

[3]F. H. Harbison, "The development of human resources. An analytical outline". From *Economic Development in Africa,* edited by E. F. Jackson, Basil Blackwell, 1965, p. 71.

[4]A. A. Liveright and N. Maygood, eds. *The Exeter Papers,* Boston, 1969, p. 9.

[5]P. H. Bertelsen, "Adult Education: a Postion Paper", unpublished report to Unesco, 1974, p. 4.

[6]Draft Recommendation on the Development of Adult Education, Unesco, Paris, 1976, p.2.

cational processes, whatever the content, level and method, whether formal or otherwise, whether they prolong or replace initial education in schools, colleges and universities as well as in apprenticeship, whereby persons regarded as adult by the society to which they belong develop their abilities, enrich their knowledge, improve their technical or professional qualifications and bring about changes in their attitude or behaviour in the twofold perspective of full personal development and participation in balanced and independent social, economic and cultural development." These definitions, embracing the dual purposes of achieving individual self-fulfilment and increasing social participation, lay to rest the notion that adult education is purely concerned with what were once regarded as non-vocational activities. The term non-vocational is in any case meaningless, since a subject is vocational or non-vocational entirely according to the motive of the learner for studying it. Adult education embraces all forms of educative experiences needed by men and women according to their varying interests and requirements, at their differing levels of comprehension and ability, and in their changing roles and responsibilities throughout life.

"Adult" Education

There is still the necessity of commenting on the word "adult". Since most third world countries are unable for a variety of reasons to provide school places for more than a proportion of their young people, there will be many youths who are desirous of starting or continuing with their education but are outside the formal system. Such people would not normally be classified as being adults. They are, however, in the world of work and have a different approach to life and society from pupils in school. They may be young in years but nevertheless they are beginning to experience the pressures of adult life. They should be given every encouragement to continue their learning. Of course there are some educational activities which are primarily the concern and interest of more mature minds, but in many cases chronological age is not such an important factor. The imbalance in the population structure of most developing countries, with a heavy concentration of people under 20 years of age, makes youths an especially important age group for which provision in adult education must be made.

Non-formal Education

T¹ These comments on the age of participants brings up a more fundamental issue. In most third world countries there will be a proportion, often quite large, of the population who will never enter the formal system of education. This will be for a variety of reasons. Insufficient resources to provide school places; negative social attitudes to education, especially regarding girls; a migratory way of life; these and other causes mean that there will be many people outside the formal system, but for whom some educational provision will have to be made which does not entail long-term, full-time entry into a scholastic institution.

To avoid any ambiguity in the use of the word adult, the term non-formal education is being substituted. Coombs defines non-formal education as "any organized, systematic, educational activity carried on outside the framework of the formal system to provide selected types of learning to particular subgroups in the population, adults as well as children".[7] Thus non-formal education is seen as being the essential complement to formal education, described as being "the highly institutionalised, chronologically graded and hierarchically structured education system spanning lower primary school and the upper reaches of the university".[8]

The term non-formal education is not wholly satisfactory. It is negative, likely to be confused with informal education which is a form of teaching/learning experience and suggests that all activities should take place outside the formal institutions of education which, of course, is not the case. It has, however, had the crucially important effect of drawing attention to the many inadequacies of the formal system and the necessity of providing the essential complement to it, namely relevant educative experiences for those untouched by the system as well as those who by reason of age are outside the purview of the formal educationist. The significance of non-formal education, of which adult education as defined in this chapter constitutes a major part, is eloquently illustrated in Diagram 1.

The advent of the term non-formal education has occurred at the

---

[7]P. H. Coombs with Manzoor Ahmed, *Attacking Rural Poverty,* Johns Hopkins University Press, 1974, p. 8.

[8]*Ibid.,* p. 8.

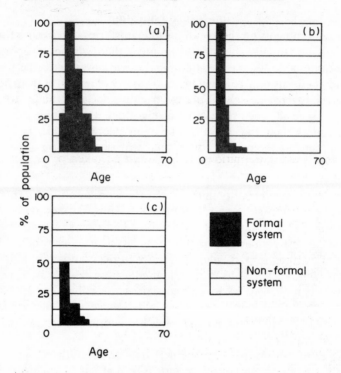

DIAGRAM 1. The respective contributions of formal and non-formal
systems to education.

Three examples of educational systems, (a)—highly developed formal system, (b)—
moderately developed formal system, (c)—formal system of many third world countries.

time when there is no longer any need to argue about its importance.
The day for which adult educationists have been preparing has now
arrived. The message of the Montreal Declaration on Adult Education
"that adult education has become of such importance for man's survival and happiness that a new attitude towards it is needed"[9] is now
accepted, at any rate in theory. The principle is recognized; if the past
25 years have been the time when adult education had to strive for and

[9]Educational Studies and Documents No. 46, Second Unesco World Conference
on Adult Education, Declaration of the Montreal World Conference on Adult Education,
Unesco, 1963, p. 11. The Declaration is reprinted as Appendix A to this book.

finally obtain recognition as an equal partner in education, the next quarter century should be the time when the theory is translated into practice. The abundance of pronouncements on the importance of adult education should now give place to carefully thought-out plans of implementation, a task which has to be undertaken individually in each country, since no two are precisely the same.

Some Other Terms

Before leaving definitions, note should be taken of certain other terms in current use over which there may be some confusion. Lifelong education (education permanente) refers to the concept of education being a continuing process throughout life, from the cradle to the grave as Muslims are admonished by the Prophet to perform. The significance of this approach is gradually being perceived since it has implications not only for adult education but also for the content of and approach to formal education. If people are really given the opportunity of continuing education, school curricula, methods and processes must clearly be designed as a prelude to the learning which will take place later in life.

Recurrent education is used to refer to the need for people of post-school age to be able to make repeated (recurrent) entrances and exits from institutions in the formal system, previously regarded as being primarily, and sometimes exclusively, for those still within the system. Thus recurrent education describes a mode of operation for a form of adult education.

Out-of-school education is a term which some use as though it is the same as adult education. This is a dangerous practice since much adult and non-formal education will take place in schools and other institutions of the formal system.

Training

It may be unnecessary to stress again that adult education, as now most commonly defined, includes skill training which was once regarded as a wholly distinct activity from education. It is true that training refers to learning particular actions, such as how to drive a 'bus or construct an electrical current, whereas education is the inculcation of mental and physical nimbleness and of knowledge.[10] But most training contains an educational component since the recipient needs to have background if the training is to be successful. Indeed the short-comings of training without education may be hidden until something unusual occurs, and the person has no ability to face and tackle a problem which has not actually been taught and which requires some faculty for logical reasoning.

Community Development

This term is used to describe both an aspect of adult education as well as an approach to adult learning through community involvement and action, a method now universally accepted and applied. "Community development covers all forms of development activity in the field and has been described as a movement to secure the active co-operation of the people of each community in programmes designed to raise the standard of living and to promote development in all its forms. . . . Community development thus covers all the forms of betterment required by the community in the areas in which its members reside."[11]

The Aim of Adult Education

The primary aim of adult education is to help each individual man, woman and youth make the best of life. No system of adult education can do all that is needed; not every want can be met and priorities will have to be established, as will be discussed in a later chapter. Nevertheless, the aim should not be obscured of seeking to help each individual to develop their potentialities to the fullest extent possible. As the President of Tanzania, J. K. Nyerere, said: "the education provided must therefore encourage the development in each citizen of three things; an enquiring mind; an ability to learn from what others do, and reject or adapt it to his own needs; and a basic confidence in his own position as a free and equal member of the society, who values

---

[10]L. J. Lewis and A. J. Coveridge, *The Management of Education,* Pall Mall, London, 1965, p.30.

[11]Peter du Santoy, *Community Development in Ghana,* Oxford University Press, 1958, p.31.

others and is valued by them for what he does and not for what he obtains".[12]

This is both a wise and a bold statement. The three ingredients signify the liberation of man from ignorance, not to become a thoughtless robot passively receiving and executing orders without dissent, but to be a creative, sensitive, aware, participating member of society, making the fullest contribution of which he or she is capable. A country which adopts such aims should not fear the consequences when its citizens have been lifted from enslavement and transformed into inquiring and confident individuals. For it will be better to live with any discomfort which stems from sincere criticism to the illusory safety of imposed conformity.

For it has to be recognized that in the process of liberation, honest differences of opinion may emerge. As Simmons has expressed it "unfortunately the goals of the different groups are often rather vague, may be misunderstood and are sometimes mutually contradictory. While an individual may be trying to increase his socio-economic mobility by attending a course, his government may rather be using the course to achieve its goal of maintaining either social stability or political stability."[13]

It is at this point that adult education has to be seen in its political context, for the full development of a system whereby adults can obtain educational nourishment must inevitably have political repercussions. It is for this reason that adult education is often regarded with apprehension by politicians. For no one should be in any doubt about the transforming power which adult education can have on individuals, communities and nations. Once people have been encouraged to think, life will never be the same again; and the thought processes stimulated possibly in some apparently narrow field will overspill into a regeneration of the whole of living and affect every part of it. This has been shown in the literacy teaching methods advocated by Paolo Frere; by learning the skills of reading and writing as a result of discussion of key words which refer to the social, and

[12]J. K. Nyerere, *Education for Self-reliance,* quoted in *Adult Education Handbook,* Tanzania Publishing House, 1973, p. 247.

[13]J. L. Simmons, "Towards an Evaluation of Literacy and Adult Education in Developing Countries", unpublished: Department of Economics and Graduate School of Education, Harvard University, 1970, p. 22.

economic condition of the participants, the whole of life is revealed with the inevitable political ramifications which every problem contains.

An International Instrument

Following its Third International Conference on adult education in Tokyo, 1972, Unesco, with the unanimous consent of its Member States, has published an international instrument on adult education.[14] The fact that the position has now been reached where it is deemed essential to make a pronouncement of this kind is both encouraging and significant. It has been stated previously that adult education has at long last recovered the status which earlier teachers from Socrates to Comenius accorded to it. That it is now felt necessary to draw up guidelines for it signifies that the international community recognizes it to be of central importance, not only to the life of each country individually but also collectively to the world as a whole. This is indeed a significant moment in the life of adult education.

The full text of the proposed instrument is given as an appendix (B) to this volume. It has a section on the aims of adult education and includes the following:

developing a critical understanding of major contemporary
   problems and social changes...;
developing the aptitude for acquiring ... new knowledge,
   qualifications, attitudes or forms of behaviour ...,
ensuring the individual's conscious and effective incorporation
   into the world of work . . .;
promoting increased awareness of the relationship between people
   and their physical and cultural environment ...;
creating an understanding of and respect for the diversity of
   customs and cultures. . . .[15]

National Aims for Adult Education

These aims are inevitably broad and global in their implications. It is essential therefore that each country should ennunciate its own set

---

[14]Draft Recommendation on the **Development of Adult Education,** Unesco, Paris, 1976.

[15]*Ibid.,* p. 2 (annex 1).

of aims both for education as a whole and also specifically for adult and non-formal education. Such a pronouncement will provide the setting in which the development of adult education can take place; it will help to establish a positive climate of thought towards this branch of education and it will indicate the significance which government attaches to it.

In some countries the objectives are expressed in a manner indicating the role of adult education in the political context of the country. Thus the stated aims in Tanzania[16] are (i) to keep up with new knowledge, (ii) to fill the education gap, (iii) to be a basis for social change and (iv) for the mobilization of the people for development.

To these may be added aims which tend to be more specifically functional in their elaboration. An example of this kind comes from Nigeria[17] where the national objectives in adult education were cited as being:

(i) to provide functional literacy education for adults who have never had the advantage of any formal education;

(ii) to provide functional remedial education for those young people who prematurely dropped out of the formal school system;

(iii) to provide further education for different categories of completers of the formal education system in order to improve their basic knowledge and skills;

(iv) to provide in-service, on-the-job, vocational and professional training for different categories of workers and professionals in order to improve their skills;

(v) to give the adult citizen of the country the necessary aesthetic, cultural and civic education for public enlightenment.

Whichever way the national aims for adult education are stated, it is of the utmost importance that such a pronouncement is made and given legal sanction through legislation. It is of little use paying lip-service to the importance of adult and non-formal education in the development of a country without following this up with the fullest possible

---

[16]*Adult Education Handbook,* edited by the Institute of Adult Education, Tanzania Publishing House, Dar-es-Salaam, 1973, pp 3-6.

[17]Report of the Seminar on a National Policy on Education, Government printers, Lagos, Nigeria, 1973, para. 77.

support. A first task in this direction is a strong and unequivocal statement by government, followed by the resources needed to implement whatever has been proposed.

Planning and Flexibility

To achieve such objectives, however, there has to be a balance between flexibility and planning. Any plan must take full account not only of the variety of human needs to be met but also of the constant probability of the unknown taking place. "We do not quite know what problems will arise, but we know that we shall need alert and skilled people to meet them. . . ."[18]

At the same time there must be planning, an element which has been conspicuously absent in so many schemes of adult education. The pace and direction of development of under-developed countries will depend on the extent to which ". . . the available pool of science and technology, mainly embodied in persons, is applied to the solution of problems of production and distribution in those countries. It is at this point that the problem of adult education as a factor in economic development emerges."[19] Such action cannot be left to haphazard chance.

It can be reasonably argued that there is a sufficient store of technical knowledge to overcome the majority of the more pressing problems with which developing countries are beset. The crucial issue now lies with the people, whose human and social values often impede the implementation of plans for development. Poverty of two kinds is the main obstacle. "Poverty is not only a physical state, relative to a variety of questionable indicators; it is a state of mind inevitably linked to and embodied in ones own sense of worth and wellbeing.[20] "From

[18]P. H. Bertelsen, "Problems and priorities in adult education". From *Development and Adult Education in Africa,* edited by Carl Gosta Widstrand, Scandinavian Institute of African Studies, 1965, p. 34.

[19]Godfrey Landuer, "Adult education and economic development". From *Development and Adult Education in Africa,* edited by Carl Gosta Distrand, Scandinavian Institute of African Studies, 1965, p. 18.

[20]C. J. Roberts and E. E. Jacobson, Professor of the City, paper presented to National University Extension Association, Albuquerque, New Mexico, 1966, pp. 20-21.

whichever angle we view the factors which hinder progress . . . we are brought back in the end to two root causes; the poverty of much of rural Africa and the lack of adequate education."[21] Adult education is clearly a factor concerned with both.

---

[21]T. R. Batten, *Problems of African Development,* Part II, Oxford University Press, 1960, p. 61.

The chapter will be divided into the following parts:

CHAPTER 2

Programme

Introduction

Carefully worded definitions and persuasive exhortations concerning the importance of adult and non-formal education are meaningless unless they result in improving both the quality and quantity of the learning experiences which are available to men, women and youths. Thus discussion on the content of adult education and what are the essentials to be incorporated in the programme are at the heart of the matter. For it is at this point that the skeleton of theory is given the necessary flesh before it can live. To press the anatomical analogy one step further, the subsequent chapters in this book are all to do with who does it and how, what are currently called the "delivery systems". These are the blood which flow through the body and give life.

This chapter will be divided into the following parts. First, before there can be any useful discussion on content it is essential to have made a calculation of the likely areas of need. These needs will, of course, vary from one country to another, as well as between individuals and communities within a country, as also from time to time. The discussion here will be limited to providing a general framework of needs which will require national and local adaptation.

Secondly, consideration will be given to the potential participants. Who they are, what their motivations are to learn, and whether there are any significant groups who might otherwise be overlooked. From a consideration of these two items, needs and target groups, there will then be a consideration of priorities since clearly no country is going to be in a position to do everything for everybody.

At this point the likely content of each of the major areas of work which have been proposed will be considered and the chapter will conclude with some theoretical case studies to indicate how all of this might plan out in the lives of men and women, the point of the whole exercise.

Likely Types of Need

What is it that men, women and youths are likely to look for from adult education? This is a difficult question since it is never easy to be able to discern what are the real needs of an individual or a community. Spoken needs may not necessarily be the actual ones, and yet it is only by finding where the truth really lies that relevant and purposeful programmes can be put together.

Nevertheless certain areas of need have recurred in so many different environments that it is possible to indicate what they are and to be able to propose a classification of programme types. It must be emphasized that such a classification merely indicates areas of activity: it in no way determines content which has to be done in the context of individual communities and nations.

There have been several classifications of the field. Liveright and Haygood[1] proposed the following five divisions for adult education:
1. Remedial, that is making good the deficiencies many experience through a curtailed or non-existent period of formal schooling.
2. Vocational, technical and professional competence. This is either preparation for work or the recurrent need for up-dating and refreshing.
3. Health, welfare and family life, including guidance about physical and mental health, family problems, parenthood, social security and consumer education.
4. Civic, political and community competence, including instruction about national and international matters.
5. Self-fulfilment, which embraces all aspects of education undertaken solely for the enjoyment of the individual.

Prosser[2] has suggested a four-fold division of adult education into:
1. formal, that is providing adults with the possibility of obtaining the paper qualifications which they were unable to get at school;
2. fundamental or foundation education, which includes literacy and community development;

---

[1]Liveright and Haygood, Eds., *The Exeter Papers,* Boston, 1969, p. 8.

[2]R. Prosser, *Adult Education for Developing Countries,* East African Publishing House, Nairobi, 1969, pp. 9-15.

3. liberal, with which is included political and social education as well as education for self-fulfilment;
4. vocational education.

The writer[3] has postulated a simpler classification, using the following three main divisions of:

1. General education, that is the essential educational background which is required by the individual to perform his/her tasks adequately. For some this will be at the basic level of literacy, for others a primary or secondary leaving certificate, and for others a university degree.
2. Vocational training, whether it be in a technical, commercial or professional subject, and at whatever level.
3. Civic and social education, giving to each individual the chance to understand the society and world in which they live, and to experience the satisfaction derived from self-fulfilment.

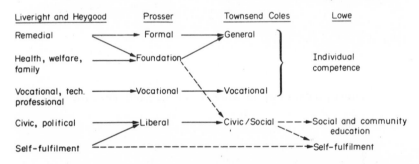

DIAGRAM 2   To illustrate the classifications of content mentioned in this chapter.

Whatever title is attached to each particular aspect, and of course there is a certain amount of overlapping between categories, there is the common thread running through them all. Man desires educational support in both his economic and social roles and both must be met. Another way of putting this has been suggested by Lowe[4] who

---

[3]E. K. Townsend Coles, *Adult Education in Developing Countries,* Pergamon Press, 1968, pp. 27 ff.

[4]John Lowe, *Learning Opportunities for Adults,* unpublished paper for OECD, Paris, 1975, p. 16.

postulates three types of need in adult education, namely, for the improvement of individual competences, for social and community education and for self-fulfilment. It will be readily perceived how these three needs fit into the classifications of types described above.

The main value in drawing up a table of likely areas of adult education is to ensure that each is given due consideration when it comes to formulating programmes of action. The question of priorities will be discussed later, but for the time being the point should be emphasized that only by an examination of the whole scope of adult education is it possible to make wise decisions as to which area warrants more consideration than another. Indeed a first task of any authority charged with the responsibility of developing a national system of adult education should be to formulate a classification of types which best fits the particular situation; arising from such a survey decisions on what action to take can be made, bearing in mind the vital caveat that these decisions must spring from the participants themselves. It is thus of prime importance to know the potential participants both as individuals and in communities and the survey mentioned above must therefore primarily be one of seeking to discern what it is that people are in need of.

The Participants
Division according to educational level
This review of the participants will be made in three ways, all of which are helpful when considering the content of the programme. In the first case groupings can be distinguished according to the level of formal education which individuals have received and from this examination likely needs may be derived. A classification of this kind is shown in Table 1.[5]

Many communities will, of course, have representatives of all four categories listed in the table, and there will consequently arise a need to be meeting differing requirements at the same time. A classification such as this does not attempt to offer any more than an indication of the types of adult education which will be needed; it gives neither a quantitative assessment of the numbers involved in each group, nor

[5]Adapted from Roy Prosser, *Adult Education for Developing Countries*, p. 17.

TABLE 1. *Classification of needs according to educational level*

Educational level	General			Vocational		Civic
	Basic	Intermediate	Higher	Basic	Higher	
No formal education	Yes			Yes		Yes
Primary education	?	Yes		Yes	?	Yes
Secondary education			Yes	?	Yes	Yes
Tertiary education				Yes	Yes	Yes

does it help in the determination of priorities. Nevertheless, it is useful in giving a readily understood picture of the main categories of need.

Motivation

Another way of looking at people is to seek to understand each individual's motive for wanting to learn. If this can be done then the learning experience—that is, the programme—can be made so much more relevant and the approach more in line with the learner's wishes. A good class teacher of adults will always seek to know why each individual member of the group is present, since only by so doing can the person be most profitably helped. When it comes to gauging motives in whole communities the task is more complicated and therefore much harder.

It has been repeatedly shown that the spoken motive is not necessarily the dominant one; often there are real or imaginary reasons for concealing the truth. This may be particularly the case in small communities, where there will be strong pressures for people to conform, and all to appear to have the same motive for their actions. Differences may only emerge when people feel confident enough to be able to speak their own minds.

In those aspects of adult education which lead to some form of public recognition there may be a variety of reasons why such studies are undertaken, amongst them being the following:

1. The qualification is essential for a better job.
2. The qualification is essential in order that higher studies (say, to a university) may be embarked upon.
3. The work for the qualification is of interest and use.
4. The work involved will enable the person to keep abreast with his children in formal education.

If an examination is made of the first and second motives above, it will be seen that those studying in order to get a better job may well prefer the content to be wholly vocationally oriented, whereas those seeking higher education may well want a more "academic" experience. This is a simple illustration of how participant motives will have an effect on the content of programmes, and consequently how important it is to ensure that programmes arise from the people, and not the people having programmes imposed upon them.

This last point is especially important when motives are being sought for participation in the more informal activities which do not lead to a qualification. Here again it is crucially important to try to understand why people want to learn since this will be the basis on which the programme is constructed.

Homogeneous groups

There are in every community distinct groups, the most obvious division being between men and women, each representing about fifty per cent of the population in most countries.

Women

It is a distressing fact that three-quarters of the way through the twentieth century it is still necessary to emphasize the need to ensure that women can participate in all forms of adult education; a need highlighted by the somewhat gratitious insult which the largely male-dominated United Nations felt compelled to make by designating 1975 as "International Women's Year". However, facts have to be faced and it has to be admitted that over much of the world women are still a deprived group. One response to this situation is to make special provision for them in subjects deemed to be of particular concern, and especially in those fields known as "domestic science" and "home economics". This provision is often very necessary and since women may be able to participate in educational activities at times different from men, it is natural that the idea of women's education as a thing distinct from that for men should have grown up. Furthermore, there are societies where for social reasons combined activities for men and women are not as yet possible. Nevertheless the education of women ought not be to be regarded as something which is achieved solely by the provision of programmes in "women's subjects". The vital thing is to ensure that women participate in all aspects of adult education, and are brought fully into the economic, political, cultural and social life of a nation. If this provision has to be made separately from that for men because of the social and cultural climate of the country, then it must be so; at best, however, men and women should be enabled to study together since it is in this way that respect and understanding for each other will be fostered and women brought fully into the main-stream of thought in a country, at whatever level, national or local.

Youths

A second important group requiring special attention are youths, the 15-25 age group for whom adult and non-formal education will be their main channel of advancement, even though they may not be of adult age. There are usually strong reasons—pedagogical as well as social—for not mixing young with old (though there may well be ex-ceptions to this and it should not be regarded as a rigid rule under all circumstances). There are also aspects of adult education likely to be of especial concern to younger people, and this may be particularly so in vocational training. It is, therefore, extremely important that due care should be taken to ensure that the needs of youth are taken properly into account when designing programmes of adult education.

Groups with common interests

The first classification, according to educational level, distinguished between those with no formal education and those who terminated at the primary, secondary and tertiary levels. Within each of these, and usually cross-cutting over the boundaries of them, there will be sig-nificant groups of people with common interests who will need special provision and for whom common educational activities should be provided. These groups may be concerned with a particular vocational activity; members of a co-operative, for example, may include people from several educational levels but who should be able to learn to-gether the skills required for their work. Some of these groupings will arise from political, trade union, religious and social activities, where again those sharing a common interest will want to join together for their educational advancement.

Many vocationally oriented groups are very obvious to spot. People in the armed forces and the police, for example, working under a particular discipline and often living in segregated quarters, are readily cited examples. There are also nurses, doctors, farmers and other groups sizeable enough to be visible and unlikely to be forgotten. Less likely to be given adequate consideration are prisoners.

Forgotten groups

There are, however, groups who for one reason or another may be forgotten and become virtually deprived of the possibility of continuing with their education. In most third world countries the need to give especial regard for illiterate people does not need stressing; it is possible, however, that even these less fortunate people can be overlooked and this is likely to be particularly true in urban communities, where numerically they may not constitute so large a proportion of the population. At the other end of the educational ladder, there are those who have had a considerable amount of formal education but who are compelled, by reason of their work, to live in isolated and only partially literate environments. Such people constitute a valuable asset in the development of a country on whom considerable financial outlay has been made to give them secondary and tertiary levels of education. They are likely to lose their intellectual vigour and their contribution to society will correspondingly diminish unless they are encouraged to continue with their education.

One such group found universally are the aged who, though economically less active than those younger, nevertheless wield great social and moral influence. In many communities their contact with the young is as significant as that of parents and in the political life of countries their voice is often the most highly regarded. Then there are the physically and mentally handicapped whose lot can be greatly improved, and their contribution to society increased, if some special attention is paid to their needs. It is perhaps significant that it is only very recently that what claims to be the first Adult Education College for the Handicapped[6] should have been established. This may be a

---

[6]Prospect Hall, Adult Education College, England.

facility which third world countries cannot yet afford; nevertheless the needs of the handicapped should not be neglected. In many countries there are ethnic minorities which demand special consideration; migrant workers needing language instruction, and others lacking the necessary basic education to participate fully in the life of the country.

Shift workers

There are then those who by the nature of their work may have to be provided with special arrangements. The fact that many women are often able to take part in educational activities by reason of their domestic and economic duties only at particular times has already been referred to. In a sense they constitute the biggest group of "shift" workers in the community. Farmers also have to work to a special time-table and programmes in rural areas must clearly fit into the rhythm of life dictated by their daily and seasonal obligations. Nomadic peoples have been a very neglected group in part because of the obvious difficulties in making suitable provision for them. And yet in countries such as Somalia they constitute a major proportion of the population. Clearly they can only be expected to countenance the idea of educational activities at moments when the pressure of keeping themselves and their flocks alive is at its least.

Summary of Classifications

Thus the potential clientele for adult education can be viewed in three ways. One is a classification by level of education, a useful if somewhat simple division. The next is by motivation; an essential exercise if the learner is to be properly understood and helped; one which is most useful in respect of general education and skill training, but which may be too rigid when civic education is being considered. The third approach is by considering likely groupings in the community for whom adult education will have some special significance.

The Problem of Priorities

Clearly it will not be possible for all the educational requirements of all members of the community to be met, at any rate through provision for which some or all of the cost has to be found from public funds. None of the so-called developed countries have reached this stage, and it is certainly beyond the capacity of all third world countries to do so. Nor indeed should they be encouraged to attempt it; effort spread too thinly over many facets will simply be dissipated and fail to make the necessary impact. Funds thus spent are mostly wasted, a statement which sadly summarizes much of the work undertaken in the field of literacy.

The question of priorities, however, raises many issues—political, social and ethical. It will be the intention of all democratic countries to do the best possible for the maximum number; it will not be the desire to allow any group or section to appear to be forgotten.

It is here that the significance of a statement of national policy will be appreciated, for it is first and foremost at the national level that countries must determine their priorities, and consequently how funds are to be apportioned. Such apportionment, however, must be sufficiently flexible to allow for particular local variants. Thus, for example, whilst it may be agreed to emphasize the needs of rural dwellers, the requirements of those living in urban areas ought not to be wholly disregarded.[7] In drawing up priorities there must be some concern for all sections of the community as well as for all aspects of adult education. It is tempting to place all the emphasis on those areas which are obviously closely connected with economic development and, indeed, high priority should be given to them. But man is not only an economic being, he is also a member of society with social obligations, and to disregard wholly this side of his development is likely to cause frustration and to undermine what is being done in the economic sphere. It is important to enable all, and particularly those with only a limited educational background, to become fully participating members of the body politic and this involves more than opportunities for skill training.

An illustration of a country making a choice to direct much of its efforts on one target group comes from India. Faced with the gigantic task of a nation with 210 million illiterate people over 15 years of age, the government has decided to concentrate on those in the 15-25 age group, 90 million young people in all of whom 52 million are illiterate.

[7]It is worth noting that the World Bank which previously had been concentrating attention on the rural areas has announced in its Annual Report for 1975 that complementary attention must now be given to the urban areas.

The approach is to design a special curriculum related to their needs which will include information and knowledge of the living environment, introductory occupational skills, basic knowledge for understanding the socio-economic, scientific and technological changes taking place and elementary principles of health, hygiene and nutrition. Special teaching materials will be prepared, the full basic course taking about 350 hours to complete. This massive scheme forms part of the current national development plan.[8]

Indeed, it is at the point of determining priorities that it is most important for educationists and planners to be in regular and close contact. It is sadly still the rule rather than the exception for adult educationists to be excluded from discussions leading to the formulation of national plans for development and the fault by no means rests exclusively with the planners. Adult educationists are often not sufficiently articulate, nor have conceived their plans with sufficient focus, to warrant being considered. This, however, is a regrettable state of affairs since clearly in formulating development plans the continuing education of the adult public must inevitably figure prominently. To leave such decisions to people without professional competence in adult education would be akin to planning a medical service without consulting surgeons and physicians.

The Content of Adult Education

This introduction to the programme now enables a closer inspection to be made of the various aspects to be considered, bearing in mind the clientele to be served and the need to determine priorities. The subject will be divided into the three areas of general education, vocational training and civic and social education. It must again be emphasized, however, that the handling of content in this way is being done purely for the sake of convenience. It is usually not the actual content of the programme which determines the category it should be in but the motive of the learner to participate in the process. Subjects cannot be classified as being vocational or non-vocational since they may well be both. An aspiring carpenter joins a class on woodwork; for him it is vocational training. A householder seeks the

[8]*Non-formal Education for the Age-Group 15-25 years* by Mrs. S. Doraiswami, Directorate of Adult Education, New Delhi, 1974, pp. 3-5.

same activity as an act of social education either so that he may better undertake his responsibilities in the home or for his own gratification. Furthermore, much that is done will embrace more than one facet of adult education. The concept of polyvalence[9] is important since many diverse needs should be met. This is particularly true of general education and especially of functional literacy programmes which incorporate elements of all three of the proposed subdivisions.

With this caution in mind, it is useful to break down an examination of content in the way suggested since this makes for manageable analysis. If adult education truly embraces *all* organized educational activities for adults its content is limitless. It is, therefore, essential to provide some framework within which to make an examination, otherwise it will seem no more than a hotchpotch of activities.

General Education

This is a significant branch of adult education since it includes activities which help to provide adults with what is regarded as the essential educational background required to function effectively in the community. It thus embraces the entire spectrum of educational levels from illiteracy to tertiary provision; for some it is the chance to enjoy for the first time formal instruction; for some it is a second chance to obtain both knowledge and a qualification which they were denied at an earlier age; for some it provides a chance to continue with their studies to higher levels of learning.

A feature which is common to all sectors of general education is that the work usually leads to some recognized qualification. This is certainly true at the upper levels and in many countries it is so also for those studying at a basic level.

There is a somewhat persistent attitude among many theoretical educationists to decry the idea of people wishing to obtain paper qualifications. So many of those who indulge in this form of snobbery are themselves the recipients of higher degrees and would passionately object if their title was omitted. In a world where so much importance

---

[9]The term polyvalence is used to emphasize the need for education to be concerned with the whole of life, at home, at work and in the community. It is a restatement of the monastic ideal of learning through both intellectual and manual exertion or as the early founders of the YMCA prescribed that programmes of local Associations (Clubs) should cater for the full development of the individual in body, mind and spirit.

is attached to having some kind of verifiable recognition it is inevitable that most people will seek tangible evidence of their efforts and achievements.[10] Nor is there the slightest bit wrong with this so long as economic advancement hinges on the holding of publicly acknowledged qualifications. The important issues are to ensure that the content of what is being studied is relevant for adults and that a suitable manner of testing is adopted.

Examinations

To consider the second point first. The idea that an examination must consist primarily of written work undertaken in conditions where those participating are held incommunicado with each other is, of course, quite falacious. For certain subjects, and some age groupings, this form of testing may be appropriate. This may also be the case where some adults are concerned. It is not, however, the only form of ascertaining the level of proficiency obtained by an individual nor is it usually the best. Indeed when it is necessary to test adults rather than make an assessment over a period of time, there is much to be said for conducting the examination on more than one session and in more than one manner. This is simply because the adult is likely to have a greater sense of fear over testing than is so with children, and spreading the examination gives a chance to avoid loss of confidence.

It is essential that the adult learner should understand why a test is necessary. It is both a measure of his accomplishment and of the skill of the teacher. It is a way of transmitting to both how the learning process is going and where weaknesses, if any, lie. It is an integral part of the learning process and not an additional irritant appended to it.

Relevance of the material

Much of the opposition to general education for adults centres on the fact that so often the curricula being followed are exact replicas of the material being provided for children at schools. This practice has come about for several reasons; the curricula are ready made, the teachers

---

[10]Newspaper advertisement: "Applications are invited for a messenger post in the . . . Bank for a man with basic qualification of Cambridge School Certificate or a lesser qualification with other qualifications and experience". *L'Express,* Mauritius, 13.9.75, p. 8.

require no special preparation, the textbooks are available; it is an easy, cut-price solution. Secondly, it is possible to demonstrate equivalency; similar curricula lead to similar examinations and employers and others have no difficulty in comprehending the presumed academic level attained. Thirdly, usually the adult participants themselves are satisfied since they often hold a very conservative view of what education is all about and for many it is only what is done in schools which merits the lable of being "proper". It is not hard to understand why, therefore, the general education courses offered to adults continue to be mainly those taken from child education, however inadequate they may be for their original purpose, with sometimes only very minor modifications.

This use of child-oriented material has not been exclusively restricted to learning at those levels leading to formal examinations. Much of the earlier work done in adult literacy, and still not wholly expunged, used material written for children, calling on situations and experiences not relevant to adults.

In the following discussion on general education the need to ensure that what is being taught to adults is of relevance and interest to them will be repeatedly stressed. It is now accepted that this is essential at the basic, literacy, stage; there is still much to be done before the same principle is applied to all levels of general education for adults, and until it does there will rightly continue to be much criticism of it.

Ladders to achievement

It was stated that general education included all the steps between the initial basic level and tertiary education. In formal education a continuum from the first rung of primary schooling to the upper reaches of university scholarship is the vista held out before every child, and curricula are constructed on the basis of the ladder approach with the implied suggestion that children will start at the bottom rung and climb up as far and high as possible. This concept was created in the developed world and has been transplanted wholesale to the developing countries. The absurdity of such an approach is only now being recognized and remedied. What is the point of designing curricula on the assumption that children will stay at school long enough to move many rungs up the ladder when it is known that this is not the case?[11] This is not to deny the need for each rung to be progressively more demanding than the previous one; this must clearly be the case. The essential feature is to make each a self-contained unit so that the experience is beneficial and can be made full use of.

Precisely the same has to be said of general education for adults. It is right that there should be a ladder, with several rungs. There will be some youths and adults who will join the ladder not at its lowest point but who, having had some formal education, will be able to take a leap and commence higher up. And undoubtedly some of these will

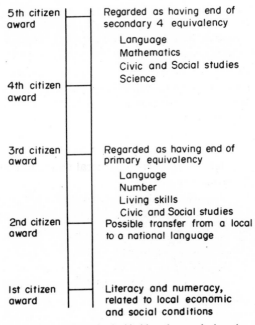

DIAGRAM 3. A hypothetical ladder of general education.

wish to go on up through various stages, to the top. For those with ability the ladder should be there, and they should be given every encouragement to progress as far up it as they can.

[11]P. Coombs, *New Paths to Learning,* UNICEF/ICED, 1973, pp. 33-35, Drop-out rates in primary level classes are, for example, 62.9 per cent Algeria, 81.3 per cent Chad, 54.9 per cent India, 80.0 per cent Bolivia.

But for many, probably the over-riding majority, their needs will be met by achieving one rung; for those without any formal schooling to have attained the first, basic, rung will be sufficient and will fulfil their aspirations; for those who have had a smattering of formal schooling, again one rung, a little higher up, will be the zenith of their ambition. And because this is looking at the situation realistically, it is essential that every section of the educational ladder should be a whole in itself and not constructed as to presuppose that people will go on to higher levels. Satisfaction must be derived from each part and this will only be so if what is learnt is complete and of direct relevance.

The actual content of the different stages in general education will be considered later in the chapter. It is important, when constructing the "adult" ladder, to make the gaps between rungs of reasonable size since the learners will also be working for a living and can devote only a fraction of their time to study. Goals which are too remote become a deterrent to learning rather than an exciting challenge.

There is also the issue of equivalency with the formal system, both because employers may demand to know the value of a course, and also the participants themselves, conditioned to think only in terms of school grades, will probably wish to do likewise. In introducing an "adult" ladder, therefore, some reference will have to be made to equivalents in the formal system.

Finally, if special courses in general education are to be introduced for adults they clearly must not be so complicated as to place an enormous additional financial burden on government. If a scheme of study for adults becomes too costly, however worthy it is educationally, it would not be put into operation. Furthermore, there is a limit to the printing capacity of countries to produce the written material required. Thus in constructing adult courses, an eye must be kept on economy.

Bridges

There must be connections between general education and the other aspects of adult education. Bridges have to be constructed so that adults can move across from one to the other as easily as to move up a ladder. One experience should open up the way for another. A place on the ladder may be the take-off point to something quite different;

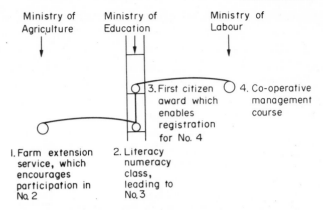

DIAGRAM 4. To illustrate the concept of ladders and bridges.

conversely access to the ladder should be as open as possible. Systems of adult education must allow for the maximum of flexibility both horizontally as well as vertically; bridges are as important as ladders.

Literacy and basic education

This is probably the best documented component of adult and non-formal education as related to the needs of developing countries. It is so universally accepted as an essential element in the programme that at times its importance has even been over-stated, the terms adult education and adult literacy being used synonymously, and other aspects relatively neglected. It cannot be gainsaid that it should be an important part of the programme in all developing countries:[12] questions only arise when other deserving facets are starved of resources.

It is unfortunate that a mystique has been allowed to develop around the subject. It was extremely important to move away from the utilization of material irrelevant to the daily life of the adult participants and to ensure that the learning experience is wholly functional in intent; that it manifestly improves the lives of the participants. This was an important step, already taken by some well in advance of the recent international efforts in this respect.

[12]In *Unesco—Literacy 1967-71* (Paris, Unesco, 1972) it is stated that in 1950 the world had 700 million illiterates in an adult population of 1579 million. In 1970 the respective figures were 783 million and 2287 million.

It is also important to have lengthened the time-scale in which events take place. True there have been examples of comparatively short campaigns producing litrate communities, regions and nations; for the majority of countries, however, illiteracy will not be eliminated by a short campaign but rather through continuing, painstaking endeavour, supported by thorough planning at national and local levels.

But in the end of the day much of the success in literacy work has been in focusing the programme on people who know they want to learn these skills and on the human approach of those undertaking the teaching. Correct methods and appropriate materials are, of course, important, as are also the continuing supply of relevant reading material and ongoing educational opportunities, for literacy has to be seen as but a beginning or as the International Commission on the Development of Education referred to it as "only a moment, an element, in adult education".[13] Literacy must thus be viewed and planned in the context of the total educational plans of a nation. But the essential pre-conditions for success are the two mentioned, to which a third needs to be added, namely the climate, social and political, in which everything takes place. As with many branches of adult education, the degree of priority and prestige given to literacy by government will in no small measure determine how enthusiastically men and women make the necessary effort and sacrifice to learn. The Cuban campaign was an early example of this; the work in Tanzania and Somalia also illustrates the same point.

Relating literacy work very specifically to the needs of the individuals concerned has to be balanced against the size of the task to be undertaken. The mass approach, properly handled, has its economic advantages and can be as effective as any other, as has been shown by the Mobral organization in Brazil.[14]

The content of basic general education

Coombs, considering the needs of children and youths, has suggested that "one must first have a clear and realistic conception of their mini-

[13]*Learning to Be,* the report of an international commission on the development of education: Unesco, Paris, 1972, p. 207.

[14]See the article on Mobral by the Development Education Centre, Toronto, in *Convergence,* Vol. VII, No. 1, 1974, pp. 61-70.

mum essential learning needs".[15] The same should be said of adults, since the purpose of basic general education for men and women is to offer them precisely that; the essential learning experience to enable them to participate in the modern world with greater confidence and improved chances of success. The ingredients Coombs recommends are the acquisition of "positive attitudes", "sufficient functional literacy and numeracy to read with comprehension a national newspaper or magazine . . ., to write a legible letter . . . and to handle important common computations . . .;" a scientific outlook and an elementary understanding of the processes of nature"; "functional knowledge and skills for earning a living"; "functional knowledge and skills for civic participation."[16]

It would be on a similar pattern that programmes of basic general education for adults should be constructed. The starting-point will vary according to the motives and interests of the learners; in the first instance in most cases it will be a matter of helping individuals and groups improve their skills whether as farmers, settled or nomadic pastralists, housewives, blacksmiths, carpenters or whatever it is that enables them to get their daily food and to live better lives. Such educative assistance will be provided in a variety of ways such as through regular visits from extension workers provided by Ministries of Agriculture, Labour, Health, Social Welfare, etc.; through short-term concentrated courses, where people in a village interested in a particular skill are given instruction by an agent who lives with the community for a short period of time; or through radio programmes.

The improvement of "functional knowledge and skills for earning a living" may well inspire some to want other things; in many cases the desire will be for literacy and numeracy; for others, improvement of living skills, that is in family life, nutrition, hygiene, child care, etc., and later the inclusion of scientific ideas and achievements; for others, it may be in civic and political education. And through these kinds of experience will develop positive attitudes to the community and the nation and the acquisition, however unconscious and rudimentary, of a scientific, inquiring outlook which will enable people to become willing and enthusiastic agents of change and development.

[15]P. Coombs, *New Paths to Learning*, UNICEF/ICED, 1973, p. 13.
[16]*Ibid.*, pp.14-15.

For it is the opening of the minds of individuals which is the basis of all true development.

Which language ?

Should adults be taught to read and write in a local vernacular language or in a national and possibly international language? In many countries such a choice has to be made.

Adults usually find it easiest to learn to read and write in their own mother tongue, and those thus taught attain functional literacy quicker than those who are taught in a national language which is not in general use in the home. The mother tongue is the natural vehicle of expression; those who never learn to read and write in it may have permanent difficulty in developing a full vocabulary in another language or in a national and possibly international language. Learning a vernacular language does not prevent a person later going on to a national language and provision for this transfer should be accommodated in the scheme of general education. The arguments for learning only a national language are that it can be used over a wider area, materials can be more economically produced, that it is especially useful for town dwellers, and that it promotes national unity. This last point is particularly important where there are many vernacular languages spoken, though it should be recognized that it is a political rather than an educational consideration. It should be remembered that with some vernacular languages, before primers can be compiled linguists must first formalize points of syntax, spelling and grammar. No directive of universal application can be given on this issue; each occasion has to be considered separately. Educationally it is best to teach in the mother tongue; political considerations, however, may well outweigh the advantages of doing this.

First citizen award

There can be no objection, if it is desired by the participants themselves, to give a designation to the first rung of the ladder and make some public recognition of it. First Citizens Award is one of many titles which might be adopted.

Going up the ladder

An individual should be able to join the ladder at any appropriate rung, the content of the various awards being constructed around the same ingredients as was advocated for the basic level.

Of course there will also be a parallel need for many activities which are wholly distinct from the scheme of general education. An obvious example is much vocational training but the same is true also for social and political education of an informal kind. These will be considered later in the chapter. The point being made at this juncture is that the curricula at all levels in the scheme of general education must be relevant to the lives of the participants, the actual composition of each rung being determined in the light of national and local needs and the interests of the learners. Progressively the work entailed is likely to take on a more formal nature though throughout there should be the same emphasis on practicability, and active learning situations such as project work and the examination of specific social, economic, environmental, political and cultural issues should feature prominently in the programme.

Public acceptance

It has been suggested that some indication should be given of the relationship of the adult scheme of general education to that in use in the formal system for children. In the hypothetical case illustrated in Diagram 3 the third award is suggested as being the equivalent to the end of primary and the fifth award to the completion of 4 years of secondary. Clearly the precise arrangements will have to be worked out in each country, to suit prevailing conditions. An essential prerequisite for the success of the scheme would be the acceptance by government and employers that citizen awards are, in every respect, as valid as their counterparts in the formal progression. Furthermore, it may be necessary to persuade potential participants that this is so also.

Entry to tertiary education

It is to be hoped that tertiary institutions, and in particular universities, will take a more flexible approach to the admission of adults than is so often the case. Demands that aspiring students must have certain school-oriented qualifications are too rigid to meet the needs of developing countries and are bound to lead to many well-deserving people being denied access to higher education. It could be argued that something akin to the fifth Citizen Award is needed for admission to ensure that the person can study at the required level and intensity. Equally important should be the record of the person as a citizen and as a worker. Indeed there is much to be said to the Tanzanian approach of requiring those to be admitted to the university first to complete a period of work in the community.

Vocational Training

No aspect of adult education is better comprehended by those in authority and consequently none is more readily supplied with human and material support than vocational training. This comment is not made carpingly; it is establishing for vocational training its rightful place. For too long educationists have tended to regard it as something second class; it is proper that in the developing countries it is recognized as being the vital component that it is.

Vocational and general education

In the discussion on general education, vocational training was mentioned from time to time. It was pointed out that for many the learning of a useful skill whereby to improve their economic potential is the first, main and possibly their only encounter with learning. There is no universal agreement on whether or not vocational training and general education should be combined. There are advocates for both approaches and probably both are right. There are times when a person wants only to be engaged in learning a vocational skill and the intrusion of any other form of educative activity will be viewed as simply an annoyance. A certain level of general education may be needed to embark on a particular course of training, but that should be sufficient. On the other hand, no one would deny that if vocational training simply results in the production of unthinking robots, it has clearly failed; trained people should be able to cope to some extent with the unexpected. Furthermore, the success of functional and polyvalent approaches at a lower level certainly testify to the desirability of combining both. As with much of adult education, dogmatic positions should be avoided. Rather situations have to be weighed up individually and suitable programmes constructed.[17]

Part of the formal system

Much vocational and professional training and retraining takes place in institutions within the formal sector of education and consequently does not come under the normally accepted rubric of adult education. These are the activities in the programme of universities, technical colleges and vocational training establishments, and mainly for registered students. Adult educationists should be aware of them though the responsibility of controlling them falls to some other department or Ministry.

The adult educationist is concerned with the myriad of activities of a less formal nature in vocational training, including the vocational component in the programmes of many voluntary community organizations.

In both rural and urban settings people want to learn useful skills. The farmer needs to learn how to grow better corn or rice; the housewife how to tend the poultry better or use the newly available packet food; the mechanic how to understand the working of some new engine; the would-be secretary how to type faster; the bricklayer how to improve his skills. These people can spare only a limited amount of time to learn; perhaps a few hours or so a week, may be some days on end, or perhaps through evening study over a longer period of time. It is important that opportunities of these kinds should be made for those who wish to learn, since the acquisition of new skills is essential if development is to take place.

Similarly, the necessity of providing recurrent opportunities for individuals to recondition what was previously learnt is now also recognized, and programmes of short-term vocational refresher courses are required in all communities and at every level.

---

[17]For a more detailed discussion see *General and Vocational Education,* a report of an international seminar held in 1973, German Commission for Unesco, Cologne, 1975.

Civic and Social Education

Just as vocational training is the most favoured part of adult education, civic and social education may sometimes be the least so, mainly because it is the hardest to organize and in the minds of some, remote from the pressing problems of economic development. The connection between a contented man in his social context and an efficient man in his economic endeavours is not always fully recognized. And yet the basis of democratic living is that all people should participate in the life of the nation and community. Ignorance is the enemy of understanding. If people are to share the burdens and responsibilities of nationhood they must be given the opportunity of learning what is expected of them.

Aspects of civic education should be incorporated in any scheme of general education. This is as would be expected since learning about ones' country is an essential element of basic general education at all levels.

But the scheme of general education is but a small contribution to what is required. Most third world countries need to tackle the problem of widespread ignorance in a much more dynamic manner by using all the skill and devices which are open to them to encourage people to be thinking about and understanding the real issues of the day.

Priority topics are likely to be connected with the political structure and economic development of the country, as well as a concern for regional and international affairs. These activities assume crucial importance in countries where the traditional patterns of government are giving way to new ones and where people have to learn their responsibilities and privileges in a changed environment. The complexities of modern living requires explanation and understanding; failure to do this may well breed frustration and resentment, especially where people feel that their rights have been tampered with without their knowledge and prior approval.

Informal programmes of social education will also be needed. The most common are likely to be of particular interest to women and will focus on the qualitative improvement of family life. Guidance in these matters will be especially needed for young mothers, since with the decreasing dependence on locally grown foodstuffs and all the material equipment which accompanies the advent of modernity their traditional tutors, mothers and grand-mothers, may be unable to fulfil their customary roles. Consumer education, in all its diverse aspects, ought also to figure in the programme for men and women alike.

It will be seen that both civic and social education are concerned with change; with the acquisition of new attitudes based on an understanding why the world of today is different from that of yesterday but without too recklessly allowing all of the traditional forms and structures to disappear. But change everywhere is now the norm and whilst both general education and vocational training will also be helping people to adapt to the revised circumstances in which they are living, it is the especial aim of informal civic and social education to enable people to become willing and sensitive co-operators in the process.

Role education[18]

An aspect of civic and social education is what is now termed role education, that is assisting people to perform better their roles in society. This is an extremely important side of adult education in the developing countries where the need to train leadership in every facet of life is widely recognized. The newly elected political representatives to local or national assemblies; those responsible for the organization of trades unions; the social worker who discovers that her work in communities involves much more than just the competence gained in the professional training course; the committee members of the local adult education centre who are called upon to consider a variety of community issues; these, and many more, are typical of the men and women upon whom the responsibility of leadership rests. They are "les animateurs", the people who infuse ideas into the community, the catalysts, the innovators.

Whether the support given to such people is done in groups or individually, it is bound to be of an informal nature. Since they will come from all walks of life and be of varying educational levels and ages, each occasion will have to be tailor-made to the requirements of the moment. There may be some theoretical approaches to leadership which are of general application, but they will only come alive when related to specific circumstances and communities.

[18]The term role education is taken from the University of Oxford Report of the Committee on Extra-Mural Studies, Oxford University, 1970.

Community development

Another example of civic education, mentioned in Chapter 1, is community development. This is the process whereby members of communities are encouraged to think about their problems and to formulate and embark upon action programmes to solve them. In a sense community development is better regarded as an approach to than a branch of adult education. The problem-solving method has been found to be stimulating and rewarding, and is widely used in many aspects of adult education. The emphasis on self-reliance—on enthusing people not just to see problems but actively through their own endeavours to be overcoming them by finding solutions should be present in all forms of adult education.

Cultural and other activities.

In danger of being neglected, but nonetheless extremely important in the healthy development of any country, are those activities which come within the term "cultural"; that is the study of literature in all its forms, of music, art, architecture, drama and dance. With the profound changes taking place in the fabric of society and the accompanying need to be learning new skills which are totally transforming former patterns of living, the significance of the cultural heritage becomes more apparent. It is the source of security, the foundation on which the new can be built, the point of pride and the focus of national unity. It is the means whereby some of the drabness and burden of life can be lightened and gaiety and creativeness enter in.

To neglect these facets would undermine the soul of a nation. The cultural roots of a people are an essential source of vitality; to starve them through disregard can only lead to a qualitative degradation of life.

People also have their own particular interests and hobbies. It may appear trivial to mention these along with all the other proposed activities. They are nevertheless important to the individuals concerned and are worthy of encouragement. Very often too they are the starting-point for further educational endeavour.

Summary of Programme Suggestions

The content of adult education is all-embracing and inevitably when looked at altogether must give the impression of being a vast web of activities. In reality, however, it is not as complicated since in any community there will be only certain selected events taking place at any given moment. The importance of the analysis made in this chapter is to ensure that due consideration is given to all the facets of adult education before a programme is embarked upon. The following headings summarize the main components which have been discussed.

1. *General education*
   A proposed ladder, each rung being a self-contained part. At the basic level the content will focus on literacy and numeracy; further up the main components will be:
   Language
   Number (Mathematics)
   Living skills (Science)
   Civic and social studies.

2. *Vocational training*
   Provision of all forms of vocational and professional training, as required.

3. *Civic and social education*
   Civic education
   Family education
   Role education and leadership training
   Community development
   Cultural pursuits
   Individual interests.

Case Studies

The following case studies illustrate the points which have been discussed in this chapter. Overleaf is given the educational history of six typical characters to be found in any community, and the recurring ways in which they participated in some form of adult education.

Personal case studies

An adult citizen, at different times in his or her life, will need various forms of educational assistance. These fall into three main categories:

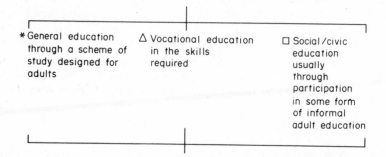

* General education through a scheme of study designed for adults

△ Vocational education in the skills required

□ Social/civic education usually through participation in some form of informal adult education

These needs will be felt in different ways and at different ages according to each individual. Participation in adult education tends to be episodic rather than consistent throughout life, as illustrated by the following case studies.

SHE   left school after only 3 years of instruction, without knowing how to read and write with confidence. She married when young and has two children. She felt the need to improve the home and she therefore joined a women's club □ and is learning homecraft. Part of the programme of the club is preparing for the First Citizen Award *. She is thus relearning how to read and write so that she can help her children as they grow up.

HE   left school at the end of primary classes. After a short break during which he worked on the family land and tended the cattle, he decided to study for a Citizens Award *. With this he was able to join a class at a nearby vocational training centre △ . On completion, he got a job as a motor mechanic. He attends the fortnightly village meeting and is also studying by correspondence for the next Citizen Award *.

SHE   is the wife of the district doctor and had a thorough general education. Now she takes part in a local women's group □ and helps to organize the town's annual drama festival □ . In order to open a shop she has attended a one-year course at the

University Business School △.

HE   left school with a good leaving certificate and was appointed to an administrative post in the civil service. First he had to attend a course for trainee administrators △ and was then posted to an out-station. To keep abreast of events he joined a university extension group □ which meets monthly in the nearby town. He has applied to the university to study for an external degree in public administration *.

SHE   left school after 2 years in secondary classes. She got a job in an office and joined a class for the Fifth Citizen Award *. When she had obtained this she was able to take up nursing as a career and she will soon complete the necessary initial training △.

HE   is now a farmer. He had practically no schooling but he realized the value of improving the productivity of his land. He was assisted by the agricultural extension officer △ and went away on a short farmer training course △. He was determined to learn how to read and write as this would help him in his work. He joined a First Citizen Award class *. When he had passed this he was elected onto. the committee of the village co-operative and attended a training course for businessmen △ run at an adult education college.

Village profile

Diagram 4 is a profile over 2 years of events to which the term adult education can be applied which took place in a village. It will be noted that the largest section is, in fact, civic and social education, with the emphasis on informal activities. It will also be seen that several agencies are involved in providing the various programmes.

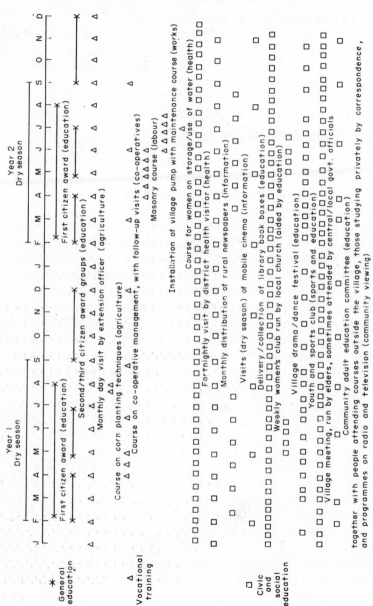

DIAGRAM 5. A village (small town) adult education profile, showing activities which took place over a two-year period.

CHAPTER 3

The Providing Agencies

Register of Providing Agencies

The implementation of a comprehensive programme of adult education demands the fullest mobilization of all the agencies which are available. It is not uncommon, however, for there to be ignorance of the full range of potential providers, with the result that resources which might be harnessed for adult education are either neglected or under-utilized. It is thus important that a register should be made of all the agencies which are or could be involved in one sort of adult education or another. Such a record ought not only to be made at the national level, but also in the smaller administrative units, since there are some agencies which are strictly local and which might be omitted if the information is compiled purely on knowledge held centrally.

Statutory and Non-statutory

One of the distinctions between the formal and the adult (non-formal) sectors of education is that whereas the former is usually controlled exclusively by the Ministry of Education, the latter is the concern of many branches of central government, together with a whole host of other agencies. The agencies of adult education thus include most ministries in government, as well as local government and many non-statutory organizations. Thus a useful classification of providers is that which distinguishes between the statutory and non-statutory agencies, as shown in Table 1.

TABLE 2. *The providers of adult education*

Statutory	Quasi-statutory	Non-statutory
Ministries:		
Education	Universities	Voluntary organizations
Labour	Mass media (Radio/TV)	Religious bodies
Health		Employers
Agriculture		Commercial undertakings
Social welfare		
Community		Trade unions
Development		Co-operatives
Youth/Sport		Political parties
Defence		Newspapers
Police		
Communications, etc.		
Local Government:		
State/Province		
District, etc.		

Other Systems of Classification

Before considering this classification and the contribution to be expected of each agency in detail, two other classifications will be mentioned.

The first is to divide the providers into categories according to their degree of involvement in adult education. This is useful in that it helps to highlight those agencies from whom most should be expected. It is particularly valuable in making some distinction within the otherwise large group known collectively as "voluntary organizations". Such a classification might divide the providers into three groups, those which have adult education as their sole concern (and this is generally a small group, not infrequently non-existent); those in which adult education is a distinct and important element; and those in which adult education is a fringe activity. Under this classification the only Ministry which would be likely to figure in the first category would be that of Community Development. The operational ministries (Education, Agriculture, etc.) would fall in the second category, as ought also universities and the mass media. Amongst the voluntary organizations there may be one or two devoted wholly to adult education, as for example a student organization such as the People's Educational Association of Ghana, but the majority are likely to be in the second category, with welfare-orientediorganizations being in the third.

The other classification makes a distinction between profit-making and non-profit making organizations, and thus draws attention to the large, and usually growing, number of agencies which retail education on the market, as opposed to those where the profit motive is not paramount, even if, in order to exist, a modest surplus of funds is accrued.

The Contribution Made by Each Providing Agency

In this chapter the first classification, that between statutory and non-statutory agencies, will be used. It has to be emphasized at the outset that there can be no universal delineation of the activities of each provider, since clearly there will be important differences between countries, according to prevailing political and social circumstances, as well as for historical reasons. Furthermore, roles are not, or should never be, permanently fixed. Rather they should be under constant review, changing with changing conditions, priorities and demands in each country. Sometimes it is proper for one agency to commence some work when it is at the experimental stage and to hand it over to another agency, often a statutory body, for continuation and expansion. An example of this would be where a university department of adult education might launch a programme as a pilot project and hand it over to another provider once its validity has been indicated. There may also be variety within a country. What is the most propitious agency in one community may not necessarily be appropriate in another.

The Agencies of Government

In most developing countries the power and authority of central government is over-riding. It is central government which controls education; it is natural, therefore, that the same degree of control will be exercised over much of adult education, at any rate over those branches in which central government is intimately involved. Indirectly, of course, governmental control extends over the whole field of adult education, since it is legislation which ultimately determines what may and may not take place.

It is a prime responsibility of central government, acting in its collective capacity, to set the overall policy for adult education, to delineate the main guidelines, enact the essential legislation and distribute responsibilities, supported by financial provision, to the various ministries. When adult education remains the responsibility of one ministry unsupported by a firm and unequivocal commitment of central government as a whole, it is unlikely to make the impact which is required. The precise form of commitment, supported by legislation, will have to be determined by each country in the light of political, social and economic conditions; that such a commitment is essential is beyond dispute. The recommendation made at the Second Unesco World Conference on Adult Education in 1961 is still valid. "The State must be concerned with adult education as an integral and essential part of the total educational system of the country . . . . In newly-developed areas . . . the government or State must take an active lead in adult education . . . (since) no government can leave the provision of adult education services to chance."[1]

Which ministry?

The government should delegate to each ministry the particular responsibilities to be undertaken, and in particular to that ministry which is selected to be the one mainly responsible for the statutory provision of adult education. Which ministry ought this to be?

It is generally accepted that the Ministry of Education should be the obvious home for adult education, thereby ensuring that the link is maintained between the formal and non-formal sectors of education, and that adult education is seen as being a part of a continuing process of education. This approach was certainly adopted at the Conference of African States on the Development of Education in Africa, held in Addis Ababa in 1961, and not, so far, officially questioned. The report says "responsibility for the promotion and development of adult education in each country should belong to the government . . . to ensure the continuity of education and its pedagogic soundness, the

---

[1]Educational Studies and Documents No. 46, *Second World Conference on Adult Education,* Unesco, 1963, p. 22.

primary responsibility . . . should rest with the Ministry of Education, in which a department of adult education will generally be desirable".[2]

A Ministry of Adult Education?

It is worth considering, however, with the growing significance of adult education, whether a separate ministry ought not to be created for it, namely a Ministry of Adult Education. The fact that this has not so far been done in any country does not entirely invalidate the arguments in its favour. One of the problems in locating adult education in the Ministry of Education is that it always is made to appear as a competitor for funds with formal education. Money spent on adults may seem to mean that less money will be available for children; and for political reasons this is an accusation no government wishes to have made against it. The separation of child and adult education into distinct ministries, both contending against other ministries for funds, and not between themselves, could eliminate any tension and make it possible for adult education to receive a more appropriate share of the national budget. Secondly, there often exists an unhappy relationship between Ministries of Education and Labour, the one being concerned with vocational education, the other with training. As far as adults are concerned, the division between education and training is largely a semantic wrangle between the professionals; what the consumer wants is preparation for a job. The establishment of a Ministry of Adult Education could make it easier to ensure that vocational training is planned jointly with the other components of adult education. Furthermore, a distinct ministry would create a career structure in adult education and thereby help in attracting and keeping good people in this branch of education.

Ministry of Education

However, the most likely ministry to be given responsibility for adult education is the Ministry of Education. There are cogent reasons why this is so. First, the Ministry of Education should be the most competent branch of government on pedagogical matters and should, therefore, be able to bring its accumulated experience to bear on problems

---

[2]*Conference of African States on the Development of Education in Africa, Final Report,* Unesco, 1961, p. 55.

connected with adults. Secondly, it has at its disposal the greatest store of professional personnel and material resources of any ministry. These must be made available for adult education. Some of the administrative and technical services are common to all fields of education, and by combining all in one ministry there might be some financial saving. Thirdly, it is essential to maintain a close relationship between the formal and non-formal systems of education. Each has much to give and learn from the other. Any ministerial divorce between child and adult education would certainly be interpreted as weakening the concept of lifelong education. Fourthly, the Ministry of Education should have links with voluntary community organizations, and is the mainspring of one of them, the Parent-Teacher Associations. For these reasons it is usual to place adult education within the jurisdiction of the Ministry of Education.

Other operational ministries such as Community Development and Agriculture are also involved in adult education and may, in terms of actual provision at the grass-roots, be as active as the Ministry of Education. It is rarely, if ever, advocated that they should have overall responsibility for adult education.

The responsibilities of the Ministry of Education

Assuming that the Ministry of Education is designated as having overall responsibility for adult education it will have to undertake the following duties.

First, it will have to foster co-operative inter-ministerial action, and be responsible for the servicing of whatever national administrative machinery is set up for this purpose, a matter discussed in the next chapter. Secondly, it will be responsible for the execution of its own activities, including the actual provision of programmes for adults. The Ministry will also be concerned with the designing of curricula and the setting of standards. It will have to make provision for the training and maintenance of personnel, the supply of teaching materials and the allocation of premises. It will maintain liaison with the mass media. It may operate a system of correspondence education and also have some responsibility for auxiliary services such as guidance and information bureaux, libraries, museums and galleries. It should be concerned about the encouragement of research and the collection of reliable statistics and other data. Finally, it will be the means whereby the non-statutory agencies are brought into a close working relationship with government. It may also be the official channel for the disbursement of statutory funds to them, as well as to individual students.

Organization of adult education in the Ministry

It must be clear from this list of duties that the Ministry will require staff who are devoted solely to work in adult education. There is, however, a divergence of views as to the best way of organizing this.

The most common solution is to set up a unit either as a separate Divison of the Ministry, or as a sub-division of another service or administrative department. Unfortunately the provision made is almost invariably too small for the tasks which are to be accomplished; adult education is dismissed to a peripheral role in the Ministry, receiving but a fraction of the resources granted to primary and secondary formal education. A second approach is to say that since adult education has links with all aspects of education—primary, secondary, tertiary, vocational, teacher-training—its personnel should be divided accordingly so that the "adult" interest in each is not neglected. This proposition sounds good in theory; in practice it means a further dilution of the impact which adult education might be making. Instead of it influencing all, it is more a question of piecemeal subjugation. A third possibility is to take adult education out of the normal administrative structure of the Ministry and give it a parastatal constitution. Those who advocate this approach see it as a means of short-circuiting the customary bureaucratic procedures of the Ministry.

Other ministries

Every branch of government should have an interest in adult education, though not necessarily as operating agencies. Quite clearly at the level of national planning and the allocation of national resources, the Ministries of Planning and Finance will be intimately concerned. The involvement of the other operational ministries (Agriculture, Health, etc.) is obvious, and to each should be remitted a clearly defined set of responsibilities, together with the resources needed to bring these to fulfilment. In each a unit designated for educational work will be required, though their size and status will vary between ministries according to the nature of the tasks to be undertaken.

Local government

The role which local government fulfils in adult education is determined largely by its place in the overall system of government of the country.

When local government is charged with the responsibility of providing educational facilities for children, and in the developing countries this is very much the exception rather than the rule, it is likely that it will have direct responsibility also for providing adult education, and thus undertake some of the duties outlined earlier for the Ministry of Education. When this is not the case, local government will play a supporting role in adult education. The forms this takes will vary, but it could include the following. First, local authorities should be able to assist with the recruitment of suitable staff for adult programmes and particularly the many part-time teachers needed. Secondly, they should help with the dissemination of information, possibly through the production of a regular local news-sheet. Thirdly, they could provide modest neighbourhood centres in which adults can study and read in comparative quiet and which are well enough lit for serious reading. Finally, they should give moral and material support for educational activities provided by locally based non-statutory organizations.

Non-statutory Providers

In most developing countries, the statutory authorities account for the biggest share of adult education; nevertheless the non-statutory providers are usually very significant, though their relative importance varies according to the political system of the country. Within the non-statutory category is a wide variety of agencies whose sole common feature is that they are not directly controlled by government. The following paragraphs describe the main agencies involved.

Voluntary organizations

This term embraces many different kinds of agencies, ranging from local hobbies and interest groups to great national and international religious and community organizations. It includes organizations for particular sectors of the community—women, youth, etc.—and for special groups such as the handicapped and the aged; those who share common interests, such as sports, cultural and occupational pursuits and community-oriented groups concerned with social issues and problems. All of these, in one way or another, have a stake in adult education, and it is in the best interests of those countries where voluntary activities such as these are encouraged, for the statutory authorities to give such support to them as is possible. Since these organizations operate on a non-profit-making basis, and rely heavily on unpaid assistance, a small financial contribution to them can reap an unexpectedly large dividend. Furthermore, participation in the life and management of a voluntary organization is a good preparation for active involvement in the affairs of the locality and nation; democratic governments wishing to encourage the development of an informed and concerned citizenry should see the value of assisting voluntary community organizations, apart from any other contribution these bodies are making to the continuing education of the adult public.

Religious organizations

Many internationally known voluntary organizations had their origins in religious bodies and to these should be added the host of activity groups which cluster round churches, mosques and temples. The remarks made about voluntary organizations in general apply equally to religious organizations; they are given special reference here because of the position of prestige and influence they hold in certain countries.

Employers and work-oriented organizations

Another group of potential providers of adult education are those associated with employment. In socialist countries employers are generally responsible for providing continuing education for their employees and they thus constitute a major provider of adult education. In other countries where there is not this form of compulsion certain employers, particularly in the larger undertakings, do make some educational provision for employees though the quality and quantity are inevitably variable. In certain cases firms employ teachers and allow employees time off from work to attend classes; others make student bursaries available. For undertakings of some size it ought always to be possible to provide modest reading and study rooms, equipped with books and newspapers.

As regard vocational skill training employers seldom have to be convinced of the need either to make provision within their own premises or to allow employees to participate in part-time, day or block release courses.

Commercial undertakings

Within this one category is comprehended a large array of providers, ranging from internationally known correspondence and language schools to back-street self-styled "colleges" in commercial and secretarial subjects; their common bond is that they all regard education as a saleable commodity, and often a very lucrative one at that, since in societies where the system of free public general education is available only to a proportion of the population there are usually many people, mostly youths, thirsting for some kind of education to help them obtain employment.

Obviously this great assortment of institutions vary very considerably in the quality of the services they offer and consequently in their usefulness to the community as a whole. Many, probably the majority, are providing an honest and much needed service, and would themselves welcome some check on the others which are not. Sadly, there are usually enough bogus concerns in every country to warrant compulsory registration and inspection of all private undertakings to ensure that at least minimum acceptable standards are being maintained, and a keen but often ignorant public is not being robbed.

It must be remembered, however, that private enterprise steps in only when there is a manifest gap in the provision being made by the statutory authorities. The best way, therefore, of countering the effects of the undesirable commercial exploitation of education in the developing countries is for governments to ensure that a better alternative is being provided.

Quasi-statutory Organizations

Some organizations cannot be classified as being wholly statutory or non-statutory, their status depending on the political climate of the country. The most important potential providers in this category are universities, the mass media, trade unions and political parties.

Universities

The attitude which a university decides to adopt towards adult education will be determined by the way in which it views its responsibilities as a whole, and this will derive in large measure from the initial source of inspiration which created the institution. In the developing countries, with the exception of some institutions in the Arab world, the majority of universities were founded by or have been patterned largely on universities in Anglophone, Frankophone or Romance countries. This division is rapidly ceasing to be valid as more and more universities are being established by the independent countries themselves. Even so, former ties, maintained through the use of a particular international language, continue to exert some effect on the planning of these new universities. Thus with regard to adult education a generalization which can be made is that whereas Anglophone countries, following British and North American practice, have expected universities to make some provision for extension activities, Frankophone and Romance speaking countries have tended not to do so, at least until very recently. There are exceptions to both these statements. Indian universities were surprisingly slow in coming into adult education; Université Nationale de Zaire, for example, has for many years had an extra-mural programme.

Those universities which have accepted adult education as a proper function, have responded to the challenge in differing ways. Those which were developed initially under British influence tended to copy the traditional pattern by establishing extra-mural departments. These brought the universities in touch with the public through the provision of classes in liberal studies. Universities, however, which were more influenced by North American thinking, such as Nsukka in Nigeria, tended to have a broader approach. An early university in Africa to re-define its adult education role was the University College of Rhodesia and Nyasaland (as it was then called) which in 1961 established an

Institute of Adult Education.[3] It was the duty of the Institute to keep under review the total educational needs of the adult community, and to assist those who were actively providing such educational facilities. A fourfold programme developed. The Institute became the place to which people naturally turned for advice on adult education; it offered various training courses in adult education leading to university qualifications; it initiated projects of investigation and research and undertook experimental programmes, and it provided classes, courses and conferences for the general public at a level and with an approach appropriate to a university. With regard to the last-named, the Institute assisted students studying privately for correspondence degrees being offered by other universities.

Many universities in Africa have since developed Institutes of Adult Education and in some cases as for example in Tanzania, the Institute is one of the main sources of material in the country, as well as offering a great many courses of preparation for adult educationists.

A seminar on university adult education in South-East Asia[4] listed the following as being the functions of a department of adult education; study and research in adult education; provision of both liberal and vocational courses; refresher courses for professional and similar specialized groups; the training of community leaders in adult education methods and techniques; the holding of conferences and seminars for the study of special problems of community and professional interest; co-operation with other organizations in adult education; advice and consultation; the general stimulation of the intellectual and cultural life of the community. The report added that universities in developing countries ought to be prepared to offer part-time degree, diploma and certificate courses.

With the increasing acceptance of continuing recurrent education, universities will be expected to pay more attention to offering short ad-hoc internal programmes for members of the adult public, and to be less obsessed with undergraduate and graduate courses of a formal kind. At the same time, universities should make themselves more accessible to adults who could benefit from a formal course, but who lack the

[3]Investment in Adults, policy statement by the Institute of Adult Education, University College of Rhodesia and Nyasaland, unpublished, 1962.

[4]J. Lowe, "University of Adult Education in South-East Asia", *International Congress of University Adult Education Journal,* Vol. V, No. 2, Dec. 1966, p. 18.

appropriate "school" qualifications or who wish to study on a part-time basis or by correspondence. The "Open" university[5] is, in fact, an institution which falls wholly within the rubric of adult education.

The developing countries cannot, and will not, tolerate the luxury of university institutions which do not play their full part in the fulfilment and acceleration of plans for national development. A department of adult education, working in relationship with the other departments of the university, is an essential tool for the realization of this ideal.

The mass media

It is general practice for the corporations controlling radio and television to be under statutory control, though through a somewhat looser arrangement than is the case with government ministries. It is clearly desirable that the controllers of the media are brought into a close relationship with those responsible for adult education. This will enable both parties to exchange ideas and for wise use to be made of these two powerful means of provision of adult education.   This matter is further discussed in Chapter 6.

In the same way it is essential that adult educationists should be in contact with film-makers—often through a government film unit—and with the proprietors of newspapers.

Trade unions and co-operatives

Both these bodies have an interest in improving the general educational level of their members, and this will be achieved partly by encouraging them to participate in programmes being offered by other agencies. But they will also wish to arrange or have arranged courses which are particularly tailor-made to their own needs. Trade unions and co-operatives require leaders who are knowledgeable of their own organizations and of the society and country in which they operate.

---

[5]The term "Open" university is used to describe a university institution which is more readily open to the whole community than is the case with the majority of conventional university institutions. It is the name of a university in the United Kingdom which provides instruction for degrees by correspondence, on radio and TV and by seminars and summer schools. For a detailed examination of this and other similar institutions, see *Open Learning: Systems and Problems in Post-secondary Education,* Norman Mackenzie, Richard Postgate and John Scupham, Unesco, Paris, 1975.

Both will require special leadership training activities at various levels from national officials to branch and village members.

Political parties

In many developing countries the political parties have taken over the position once occupied by voluntary community organizations, in that outside of government they are the most significant of the providers of adult education. This is particularly the case in one-party states. In Somalia, for example, it is the local political orientation centres which provide the main focus for many adult educational programmes, and educational work of the Tanganyika African National Union is well known, having been the inspiration behind the establishment of a residential college for adult education, Kivukoni College.

It entirely depends on the political system in force whether political parties (or the political party) have responsibilities beyond direct propaganda and proselytization for a particular cause. The position most usually found is that they do and that they provide general education as well as the more narrowly focused political education.

Principal interests of the agencies

Chapter 2 looked at the programme and this chapter has consisted of a review of the providing agencies which are available to implement these activities. The work which each provider undertakes will vary between countries and from time to time. There can be no hard and fast rules on this matter. Table 2 is a form of summary to the discussion so far. It would be valuable for every country to construct a similar table showing the likely degree of interest which each provider might take in the various aspects of the programme. Table 3 is clearly hypothetical, though it probably reflects a situation to be found in the majority of the developing countries. The subdivisions of the programme are those used in Chapter 2; the figure 3 denotes that this is likely to be a main concern; 2 a lesser interest; 1 a fringe interest and a blank suggests that this branch of the programme may be inappropriate for that particular provider.

Finally, in this chapter mention will be made of two other types of agency which though not strictly providers, nevertheless play, or could play, an important part in the development of adult education. These are student groups and international and regional organizations.

TABLE 3. *Likely involvement of the main providers in aspects of adult education*

Selected providers	Basic	General Interme-diary	Higher	Skill Basic	Skill Higher*	Civic Political	Civic Social
Ministries							
Education	3	3	3	1	1		2
Labour				3	3		
Health	3	2	1	3	3		
Agriculture	3			3	3		
Voluntary organizations	2			1		1	3
Employers	2	1	1	3	3		
Political parties	2					3	1
Mass media	2	2	2	1	1	2	3
Commercial under-takings		3	3	3	3		

*Much of this is not within the normally accepted rubric for adult education.

Student Groups and Organizations

One of the classifications mentioned earlier divided the agencies into categories according to their degree of involvement in adult education and the first of these was for organizations whose sole concern was with this branch of education. In rare cases adult education associations exist, consisting mainly of adults who are attending classes run by that association. Examples of this are the Workers' Educational Association in the United Kingdom, and in the developing countries the People's Educational Association of Ghana which is closely modelled on it.

Whether there is a need for organizations of this kind in countries where they do not exist is open to question. The two mentioned grew up in their respective countries at a time when government was doing very little in the provision of programmes, and they consequently filled a gap. The situation is now different, and the kind of work which the WEA in Britain and the PEA in Ghana do is usually supplied by some other provider.

There is, however, much to be said for encouraging student groups to develop, and these might be attached to Adult Education Centres and other places where the purpose of these groups would not be to provide programmes but rather a forum in which matters of concern to adult students can be discussed. Such groups are most likely to be locally based and oriented, though some form of national affiliation may develop.

International Organizations

There are a few voluntary, non-statutory organizations which are concerned solely with adult education. The International Federation of Workers' Associations brings together on a federal basis national workers educational movements. The International Correspondence Association is concerned with the development of correspondence education for adults. The International Congress of University Adult Education acts, as its name implies, as a means whereby universities can exchange information and ideas about adult education. All of these organizations welcome inquiries about their work.

The most recent, and potentially the most significant, of the international organizations is the International Council for Adult Education. It is not the first attempt at international co-operation amongst the non-statutory providers, but it is the first to be so broadly based, having members in every continent. Its main concern is to give an international lead in the differing aspects of adult education and it does this through the publication of a journal (*Convergence*), the holding of conferences and seminars, and being available for consultation. Its constituent members are mainly national and regional adult educational organizations, though membership is also available on an individual basis.

Non-statutory regional organizations are a comparatively new feature. They have grown out of the desire of adult educationists within a geographical area to have regular contact with each other, and to provide certain facilities such as journals, newsletters and seminars on a regional basis. The earliest of these groupings was the European Bureau of Adult Education; there is now the Asian South Pacific Bureau of Adult Education, the African Adult Education Association, the Regional Centre for Functional Literacy in Rural Areas for the Arab States and the Regional Centre for Functional Literacy in Rural Areas for Latin America.

There are several intergovernmental organizations with a direct concern for adult education. Within the United Nations Organization, the United Nations Educational Scientific and Cultural Organization (Unesco) is the body which has overall responsibility for adult education. It discharges its duties through a section devoted to adult education, though several other parts of the organization are also concerned with specific aspects of the education of adults. In the Education sector there are also units for literacy and rural development and life-long education, of obvious and very direct relevance, and several others with a somewhat lesser, but nonetheless, important connection, such as environmental and population education, together with all the branches of formal education. The interest in adult education extends to other sectors of Unesco concerned with science, culture, communications, the free-flow of information and statistics.

Though Unesco is an intergovernmental organization, it fosters close links with many international non-governmental organizations, offering them consultative status with the organization. The non-statutory bodies mentioned earlier in this section have the benefit of this link.

The adult education section supervises the Unesco regular programme for adult education, the components of which vary from one bienium to another, according to prevailing interests and the wishes of the Member States. The on-going tasks of the section include the provision of consultants to work with Member Governments, the publication, from time to time, of seminar reports, a bi-monthly "information notes", and the maintenance of a small but good documentation centre. The section was the organizing agent for the three world conferences on adult education held under Unesco auspices at Elsinore (1949), Montreal (1961) and Tokyo (1972). Unesco has regional educational offices in Bangkok, Beirut, Dakar and Santiago.

Adult education is an important element with other agencies of the United Nations. The World Health Organization is concerned with health education; the Food and Agriculture Organization with agricultural extension; the International Labour Organization with workers' education, vocational training and co-operatives; the United Nations Industrial Development Organization with industrial matters, and to these could be added the remaining agencies, since all are bound to have some educational interest within their own specialist fields.

There are several other intergovernmental organizations which have an interest in adult education. Amongst these are the Organization for African Unity, the Organization for Economic Co-operation and Development, the European Economic Community and the Council of Europe.

CHAPTER 4

Administration and Finance

Introduction

The previous chapter was an analysis of the agencies providing programmes in adult education. It was seen that very many are involved, including most of the ministries in government. It was further suggested that it is essential for one ministry to be vested with the overall responsibility for the development of adult education, the most likely choice being that of Education.

This chapter will continue the discussion on the administration of adult education, and two points in particular will be considered. The first is the need to establish a framework, at all levels, in which the various agencies can operate and which will encourage mutual cooperation between them. For such a framework to be effective, all the participating agencies will have to be able to play some part in shaping policy and deciding on what action needs to be taken. Secondly, the Ministry responsible for adult education will have to be adequately staffed to undertake the work, and the chapter will include consideration of the form which a department of adult education should take.

First Things First

At the outset, one cautionary word must be expressed. That there should be a solid framework for adult education in each country is beyond dispute. This does not mean, however, that the first step in achieving this is necessarily the establishment of a cumbersome committee structure. Indeed there are many things which need to be done which are of a far higher priority, including the appointment of trained staff at all levels in the Ministry responsible for adult education and the development of the essential ancilliary services which are known collectively as "the delivery system", and which are described in Chapters 5 and 6. Through such services it will be possible for the Ministry, at national, intermediate and local levels, to be able to offer practical assistance to the other agencies, statutory and non-statutory, and thereby create a positive climate of co-operation on which the effective working of a national framework for adult education should be based.

This caution is being voiced because in the discussion which follows it might be thought that the first and fundamental step in getting a system of adult education established is to form a committee structure. That such bodies are ultimately needed is certain. Their foundation will be more secure, however, if in the first place co-operation between agencies is encouraged by acts of mutual assistance rather than through what might seem to be the imposition of a heavy-handed, bureaucratic machine.

Keeping these introductory remarks in mind, the discussion on the administration of adult education will now proceed.

An Organizational Framework

Commentators have repeatedly stressed the lack of satisfactory administrative machinery for adult education. As a Unesco report on Guyana stated "there is no central driving force, no organizing or integrating authority to co-ordinate the diffuse activities of the many organizations which are interested in this important sphere of social development";[1] and such remarks can be found in many other educational reports. In a paper read to the inaugural meeting of the Adult Education Association of East and Central Africa in 1964, Lewis asserted that "rarely does machinery provide for more than a polite exchange of platitudes".[2] In 1973 it was still necessary to be making similar demands for an adequate framework within which adult education could function. In that year the International Symposium on Functional Literacy in the Context of Adult Education held in Berlin, made the recommendation that "in view of the need for permanent

---

[1] C. L. Germanacos, H. Wander and G. S. Congreve, *Report of the Unesco Educational Survey Mission to British Guyana,* Unesco, 1963, p. 71.

[2] L. J. Lewis, "Adult Education and Development Planning", unpublished paper, 1964, p. 2.

provision for adult education, governments should take a long-term view and establish the necessary institutions and structures".[3] Maybe adult education is now accepted as an important and integral part of education but there is still much to be done before it is firmly established in most countries within a viable organizational framework.

This framework must, of course, fit into existing statutory patterns of administration and be right for the country concerned. It follows, therefore, that there can be no overall global blueprint for adult education; each country must be considered on its own, and fashion its own system to meet its own particular requirements. There are, however, certain guidelines when considering the administration of adult education, and it is the purpose of this chapter to consider them.

In most developing countries the main providers of adult education are the statutory authorities. Nevertheless, as was pointed out in the previous chapter, the contribution in many countries made by the non-statutory organizations is very considerable, and it is essential, therefore, that some place should be found for them in the general framework. Furthermore, since participation in adult education is usually on a voluntary basis it is important that the "students" should also be able to exercise some degree of influence, and consequently also have a place within the organizational framework.

Thus the three principal guidelines in setting up a framework for adult education should be that it enables governments to carry out their stated policies in adult education; that all the agencies, non-statutory as well as statutory, should be enabled to make their fullest contribution to the work; and that the participants themselves should have a part in the decision-making process.

In its simplest form what is required is that at national level there should be an authoritative body which can advise government on the framing of policy and subsequently ensure that the tasks to be undertaken are remitted to the respective providers. Such a body will need to maintain a continuing over-view of the total development of adult education. At the other end of the scale there will have to be local machinery to ensure that activities are taking place and that the needs and aspirations of the people can be made known to higher authority. In most countries it is necessary to establish one or more

---

[3]*Functional Literacy in the Context of Adult Education.* German Foundation for International Development, 1973, p. 173.

intermediary levels of control. This administrative pattern can be illustrated as follows:

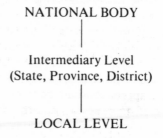

NATIONAL BODY

Intermediary Level
(State, Province, District)

LOCAL LEVEL

It is not an unimportant quibble to suggest that this diagram should also be viewed in the reverse manner, with the local level shown at the top. This would demonstrate the point that "control" in adult education has to be seen in two ways; there is control from the national level, where policy and priorities are determined and financial allocations are made. But there is also a strong element of control from the bottom, for unless the provision made is felt to be relevant and interesting by the people, the consumers, there will be no participants and hence no activities. This may be a different order of control from that exercised by national and intermediary bodies set up by the government; it is, nevertheless, a very potent form of authority and one which should not be disregarded.

National Control of Adult Education

In the previous chapter, a distinction between formal education on the one hand and adult and non-formal education on the other was noted, namely that whereas the former is the concern of one Ministry (Education), the latter is of direct interest to several branches of government, as well as to many non-statutory providers. This is obviously a complicating factor when considering composing a suitable administrative framework.

There is, however, increasing agreement that there needs to be a national body to be responsible for or concerned with the whole spectrum of adult education. The differences emerge when the question as to what form this body should take is discussed and whether it should be invested with executive responsibilities or be restricted to acting only in an advisory capacity to those agencies represented on it. A third possibility is that it should have a dual role; advisory in some aspects and executive in others.

There appear to be four approaches from which a choice has to be made. The responsibility for setting up a national body should be vested in the Ministry which has overall responsibility for adult education; a second way is to place it under the control of a consortium of ministries. A third approach would be to establish a national body entirely independent of government, and the fourth to have a dual system whereby a statutory board would retain executive control and side-by-side would be a separate advisory body on which all providers were represented. Each of these approaches will now be considered.

Single ministry

This is the simplest and most usual arrangement to be adopted. The national body for adult education is related directly to the ministry responsible for adult education, though its responsibilities extend to all the agencies which are represented on it. It thus has interministerial interests, even though administratively it is part of one ministry. This may sometimes be a cause of weakness since the one ministry may seem to act in a privileged position *vis-à-vis* the others; equally so these other ministries may treat the national body with some suspicion and resentment and not be wholly willing to work co-operatively with it. Nevertheless its simplicity as well as its direct contact with the Ministry of Education are positive factors in its favour.

Consortium of ministries

Rather than place adult education under one ministry, which must inevitably arouse suspicions on the part of other interested ministries that their sovereignty is going to be violated, a special council or committee of state may be set up under the direction of a senior member of government, and preferably one who is not immediately connected with the operational ministries. Such a person may be a Vice-President, Deputy Prime Minister, or the Minister responsible for an umbrella ministry such as Planning or Local Government. The body established would consist of a consortium of the ministries involved in adult education, and would have a constitution of its own like other parastatal institutions.

There is the obvious advantage in this arrangement in that it involves, on a basis of equality, all the ministries which provide adult education. Furthermore, if the head of the consortium is at the Vice-Presidential level, the institution will clearly enjoy considerable national prestige. Its disadvantages are that it can become no more than a forum for the exchange of ideas; divorced even from one operational ministry, it may not be able to exert enough influence to get things done. As a separate institution it will tend to lack the administrative expertise which ought to be found within the normal departments of government.

Non-statutory organization

This arrangement is only likely to be operative where there is a non-statutory organization specifically for adult education which is endowed with sufficient prestige to be able to exert leadership over the whole field of adult education. These circumstances are more likely to exist in the developed countries with a longer tradition of formal and consequently adult education than is the case in most developing countries. Such an organization may act as a forum only for the non-statutory agencies, or it may include government departments within its membership. The strength of such a body is that being non-statutory it should be less constrained and more flexible in what it can do; in practice its non-statutory status is the root of its weakness. Being outside government it is likely to be shown no more than scant attention and receive a meagre allocation of funds, if any at all.

Dual control

This can be a combination of any of the three predeeding systems. There can be some form of statutory body, of one of the kinds described, empowered to deal with government policy, finance and the implementation of certain programmes and activities. Side-by-side with this could be a second body, set up either by statutory decree or as a wholly non-statutory organization with some limited executive powers, but acting mainly in an advisory capacity to its constituent members.

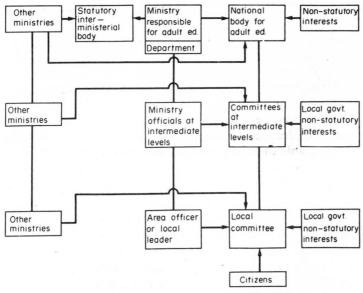

DIAGRAM 6. To illustrate a system of dual control for adult education whereby there is both a statutory inter-ministerial board and also a national body which includes all the providers.

Duties and Composition of the National Body

The discussion so far has been on the nature of the national body to be set up to be concerned with the overall development of adult education.   Its duties and composition must now be considered. Obviously these two issues are closely linked. Whilst the intent should be to make it as representative as possible of the providing agencies, the duties which are remitted to it will clearly influence both who is to be included and in what proportion will the balance be struck between statutory and non-statutory participants.   A body given the responsibility of shaping government policy and handling large sums of public money may well be constituted in such a manner as to make the statutory interests predominant over the others.   Consequently, a body accorded a purely advisory role can more safely—in the eyes of the government—be entrusted to a group of people representative of the non-statutory agencies in adult education.   Thus duties and composition are inseparably linked.

There is a further consideration over the size of the body to be set up. The need for being representative could, if taken to extremes, lead to a most unwieldy organization. If it is allowed to become too big it retards decision-making, inhibits the ability to call frequent meetings if and when particularly pressing problems arise, and adds very considerably to costs. This kind of situation needs to be avoided, and this inevitably means that there has to be some selection over the number of participants. One solution especially useful in countries where there are many equally deserving non-statutory agencies is for the national body to hold an annual national conference on adult education to which all agencies and some "students" are invited. This permits a wider public to express their views on topical issues related to adult education, and to feel they are helping to shape policy. Where this is done there is less cause for complaint if the non-statutory representation on the national body is somewhat restricted.

Clearly a first task of the national body is to act as the mouthpiece on adult education, ensuring that the significance of this branch of education is kept before the attention of government and public. It should consist of people of sufficient stature so that its pronouncements are heeded, and it must, of course, include enough women to ensure that its decisions are taken with due consideration to the needs of the whole population.

Two ministries which should be, but often are not, included in the membership of national bodies are those of Planning and Finance. If the former is omitted, adult education is likely to be neglected and its role undervalued when plans are being formulated for the economic and social development of a country. Indeed at all times there should be the closest liaison possible between planning and educational authorities in all spheres. If the latter is forgotten there is a likelihood of engendering Treasury resistance to and misunderstanding of the claims of adult education to be treated on a parity with other branches of education when it comes to allocating resources. It is thus essential that both these ministries should be included in the membership of the national body.

Should such a body be vested with executive responsibilities for adult education or ought it to remain only as a channel of consultation, advising but not giving directives to its constitutent members? There

TABLE 4. *Strengths and weaknesses of a national body endowed with either executive or advisory powers*

		Strengths		Weaknesses
Executive	1.	A strong statutory body, with power to implement its decisions	1.	Likely to reduce participation by non-statutory agencies
	2.	Greater ability to attract financial resources from the Treasury	2.	Tendency to be dictatorial over local issues
Advisory	1.	Enables fullest participation of non-statutory interests and is thus more responsive to their needs	1.	Lacks authority to implement ideas and may gradually lose prestige and drive
	2.	Allows for discussion on all aspects of adult education	2.	Likely to receive less statutory resources

are strengths and weaknesses inherent in both, as are indicated in Table 4.

There are two other possibilities to be considered: one, as has been suggested earlier, is for two bodies to be set up, and the other is for a compromise arrangement to be worked out. In the case of the former an interministerial committee would handle national policy and finance and remit to the other body matters for general discussion relating to content, methods and programming, and especially in so far as the non-statutory providers are concerned. The views of this body should be taken into account by the interministerial committee when policy is being formulated.

In the compromise solution a limited range of executive responsibilities would be referred to the national body, whilst at the same time it would act in an advisory capacity to the various constituent organizations. Such an arrangement might work out along the following lines:

Advisory:

1. To Ministries, each Ministry remaining individually responsible for its own work.

2. To non-statutory agencies, each continuing to be responsible for their own work.

Executive:

These powers might be restricted to those activities which are manifestly better organized on a national (or regional) basis by all agencies co-operatively than by each one individually. Examples of such activities, given in a rough order of ease of implementation, are the provision of

1. cultural and sporting activities and competitions (poetry, art, drama, sports, etc.);
2. certain national publications (i.e. Journal, Year Book, rural newspaper, some teaching manuals, etc.);
3. certain programmes and national campaigns, including the use of radio and television;
4. scholarships;
5. grants-in-aid to non-statutory agencies;
6. common facilities (i.e. community centres, equipment);
7. common training facilities for those who are involved in educational work in the community.

Through such a mix of advisory and executive powers, fears over loss of independence will be calmed, and the limited executive powers will help to engender a spirit of mutual confidence between the various agencies involved.

Co-ordination and Co-operation

Much is said of trying to foster better co-ordination between the providers of adult education in order to cut out duplication and make the best use of the resources which are available. This is a proper aim to pursue though it is not easy of attainment. Once an agency—statutory and non-statutory alike—has created an empire it so often falls into the human weakness of not wishing to share it with anyone else. A prime duty of the national body, however constituted, must be to encourage co-operation, which is perhaps a better goal than co-ordination. Whilst the former emphasizes sharing on the basis of continuing individuality (see Diagram 7) the latter implies, albeit often fictiously, that a take-over bid is being made and that there will be a loss of sovereignty.

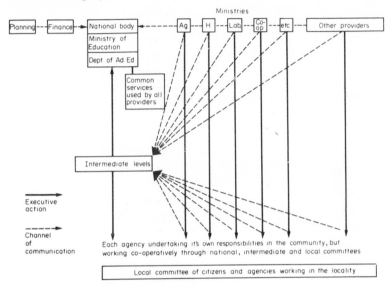

DIAGRAM 7. The concept of autonomy of and co-operation between the providers of adult education.

If, however, there is to be real co-operation between the agencies, it is essential that there should be a strong lead from government, supported by legislation, giving clear instructions to ministries not only as to their respective roles in adult education but that they must act co-operatively amongst themselves. If this is done, a reasonable climate is created in which to seek the co-operation of the non-statutory agencies; obviously, unless government ministries can demonstrate that they can work together harmoniously for the common good there is no justification to expect others to do likewise.

It is often easier to engender co-operation by starting at the grass-roots level. The absurdity of interagency rivalry is most sharply seen at the point of action; and the consumers are likely to be the people most demanding that those providing services should do so co-operatively. By enabling different providers to come together on some local project, the message of mutual assistance will gradually percolate through to the higher levels of decision-making.

Directorate for the National Body

If the national body is directly related to the Ministry responsible for adult education, it will be serviced by the relevant department in the Ministry. If, however, another formula is adopted, it will be necessary to establish a small secretariat to be concerned with the convening of meetings and the promulgation of decisions.

The Title of the National Body

Before leaving the subject of the national body, it will not be out of place to mention the desirability of choosing a title for it which is both descriptive and which comes readily off the tongue. To pay some attention to this detail will probably help in popularizing the work at all levels. There is much to be said, too, to having a symbol and a motto. These will help to promote the idea of people belonging to a movement which is striving for both individual and national betterment.

The Department in the Ministry

An effective department of adult education in the ministry responsible for adult education is the single most important resource, and the one to which the highest priority should be given for its formation. The size and scope of the department will vary from country to country, but it should certainly be accorded equal status with the departments concerned with formal education (primary, secondary and tertiary).

Within the department there should be divisions dealing with the various aspects of the work. It may not be necessary that all ten divisions to be proposed should be established; this will depend on the resources available and the tasks which have been remitted to the department. It is likely, however, that most will be needed though not necessarily each as a separate entity (see Chapter 6). The ten divisions are:

1. Administration and Finance
   Personnel; Scholarships; Grants-in-aid; Registration of activities; buildings.
2. Inspectorate
   For all adult educational activities aided by public funds and for the inspection of private institutions.
3. Training
   The training of personnel; management of training centres.
4. Material Resources
   Equipment; printing facility; educational aids.
5. Evaluation
   An evaluation unit, possible in the University rather than the Ministry.
6. Examinations and Curriculum
   For courses leading to qualifications.
7. Library Service
8. Correspondence Education Unit
9. Mass Media
   8 and 9 could be combined.
10. Reference Committees
    Committees on various aspects of adult education which have priority or deserve specialist consideration. Examples might be Literacy and Vocational Training. Reference Committees may be formed for special tasks and then disbanded.

The staff requirements of the Ministry and a suggested phased build-up of the Department are considered in Chapter 6.

Earlier it was indicated that two other ways of handling adult education in the Ministry might be to distribute personnel throughout all branches of the Ministry and secondly to set up a separate para-statal organization. It is hard to see how the former proposal could work out in practice unless at some point there is a concentration of personnel to undertake many of the duties listed above. If a para-statal institution is set up it would have a somewhat similar mix of subdivisions as for a regular department in the Ministry.

Intermediate and Local Levels of Control

Between the national and local levels there may be one or more intermediate levels of control, according to the particular needs of a country and the ex:cting administrative pattern. At these intermediate levels there will have to be adult education committees working directly under the control of the national body and representative of the agencies providing programmes. The actual composition and duties remitted to these various committees will vary according to their relative importance. In a federal country such as Nigeria, for example, the first of the intermediate levels is the State. In this case the State is the main operating agent, and is responsible for all the statutory services available to the people, including education. Since the States embrace large areas and big populations, there are other intermediate levels known variously as provinces and districts. In Greece there is a national adult education committee associated with the Ministry of

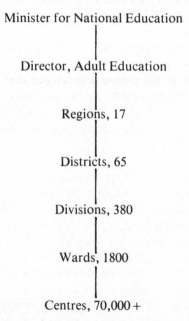

Minister for National Education

Director, Adult Education

Regions, 17

Districts, 65

Divisions, 380

Wards, 1800

Centres, 70,000 +

DIAGRAM 8. Administrative framework of adult education in Tanzania.

·Education. In each Nomos (county) there is also an adult education committee which is directly responsible for the overall control of the local adult education centres. In Tanzania there are four intermediate levels between the Ministry of National Education and the Adult Education Centres as shown in Diagram 8.[4]

However the chain of command is formed it is important to ensure that the consumers are brought in up to the highest level which is practicable and that throughout there should be a genuine two-way flow of information. It is inevitable that directives have to come down from the top; it is vitally important that the men and women participating in the activities should feel that they have a means of influencing policy and that their particular needs will not be ignored. Earlier it was suggested that in order to keep the national body within reasonable proportions it ought to organize an annual conference on adult education. Since intermediary and local committees also ought not to become too cumbersome there is much to be said, at every level of control, for keeping the formal body fairly compact and arranging annual conferences and general meetings at which the public at large can express their views.

It is at the intermediary levels that another arm of government which has not as yet been mentioned becomes significant, namely local government. It is of the utmost importance that there should be a close working relationship between the structure established for adult education and the respective strata of local government. City, town, district and village officials should not only be made aware of their educational responsibilities towards their citizens, but should be given every encouragement to become active partners in the work.

According to the number of intermediary levels and the duties remitted to them, it will be necessary to establish small service divisions reflecting some of those associated with the national directorate. Whilst these have to be planned within reasonable limitations of economy they must be adequate for the work to be done. In brief, the delivery system must be robust enough to be able to deliver the goods. This often means that at the principal intermediate level there is need

---

[4]B. L. Hall, "The Structures of Adult Education in Tanzania" (Extracted) Paper for the *Seminar on Structures of Adult Education in Developing Countries,* Nairobi, 1975, Unesco, 1975, Appendix 1.

for a small cluster of services, incorporating a modest training centre concerned with preparing the large army of part-time teachers engaged in adult education, a resource centre supplying teaching aids and acting as an equipment bank, a library service depot and possibly a subunit of the national institution for correspondence education.

It will also be necessary to have intermediary level reference committees, dealing both with those aspects which are of national concern and also with any matters which are purely regional but nonetheless deserve especial consideration.

The Local Committee

Far too little attention is paid to the establishment of good local committees. The national body receives public attention and is prestigious; but the local committee, however humble, is the vital cog in the machinery. If there is failure here, the best made national designs will come to naught.

There is a tendency sometimes to over-load local committees with *ex-officio* personalities; the Mayor, the Priest, the Headmaster and other local dignitaries are usually on the lists. There is, of course, nothing wrong with this, and indeed there is much to be gained from involving these people in adult education. At the same time, the local committee must be both energetic and representative. It is no good to crowd it with already busy people; equally it is essential that it should be a fair reflection of the community at large. This is not always an easy task; in some societies it is difficult to find enough women to serve (the idea, held by some, of a lone woman to represent female interests is a scandalous insult to 50 per cent of the community!): in others there is hesitation in bringing youths onto a committee with their elders; and in other cases significant minority groups may be overlooked. The important point is to constitute the committee so that it has both local esteem and also the strength which stems from having been democratically elected by the people. This probably means reserving certain places to be filled *ex-officio,* some for representatives of the providing agencies operating in the locality, and some (the majority) by a form of election of the consumers.

It is at the local level that another dimension of administration becomes important, that of arranging the various activities which are to take place and of registering the participants and sometimes receiving fees. Much of this work will be done by the paid officials, discussed in Chapter 6, but much also will have to be done by volunteers. For this reason it is important that administrative procedures be kept as simple as possible, and that the Ministry issues forms for the collection of data which are clear and unambiguous.

Legislation

A seminar convened by Unesco in 1975 on Stuctures of Adult Education in Developing Countries noted that "by and large, adult education lacks legalized status. Yet legislation is essential in order to delineate the operational framework in which adult education can operate . . . references are sometimes made in educational legislation to adult education, but nowhere is it legally enshrined as a human right on an equal footing with child education".[5]

The need for legislation is obvious and it is essential if a national framework of the kind discussed in this chapter is to be established. At the same time the dilemma facing governments has to be appreciated. The all-embracing nature of adult education makes it difficult to know how far one can go, within the limits imposed by financial constraints, in making it a universal public service, however desirable that may be. Equally so one does not want a system to be established which has a price-tag attached to it; something for those who can afford to pay, but not for those who cannot. Certainly, it is not unreasonable to suggest that within any legislation concerned generally with education, there should be a section relating specifically to adult education indicating that it is the intention of the government to provide such facilities for the public as are within its means.

Several countries have passed legislation on specific aspects of adult education. The seminar report quoted earlier refers to Tanzania, where steps have been taken to incorporate the ILO Convention on paid educational leave into legislation, and Nigeria where it is required of employers to pay a small percentage of their payroll expenditure towards a national fund, part of which is devoted to adult education. One piece of legislation which ought to be on the statute book of every

---

[5]Report on seminar on structures of *Adult Education in Developing Countries with Special Reference to Africa,* Unesco, 1975, p. 12.

country, as in Denmark, is that all public educational institutions, including public libraries, should be freely available for adult education.[6]

Finance: General Considerations[7]

It is only recently that serious attempts have been made to estimate the costs involved in programmes of adult and non-formal education.[8] However, in general adult education continues to be under-financed when considered in relation to the tasks to be undertaken and when compared to other sectors of education. Among the reasons for this sorry state are the following. In the first place, where there is a lack of national policy and clarity over the purposes and significance of adult education on the part of government, it is less likely to attract the resources it needs. Secondly, civil services as a whole, and Ministries of Education in particular, are controlled by people, who themselves were trained at a time when adult education was not conceived as being important. To many of them, and this comment also applies to elected representatives in parliament, the other sectors of education are the normal and proper ones and adult education no more than a peripheral frill. Such people usually need persuasion before they are willing to allocate the funds required for adult education. Thirdly, a view which is still widely held and not unconnected to the previous comment is that adult education is not a professional job but one better left to the willing, and often unpaid, volunteer amateur. Those who hold to this contention can see no necessity to make provision for full-time appointments and a career structure. Lastly there is also the

---

[6]*Ibid.*, p. 12.

[7]Much of this section is taken from "Organization and Administration of Adult Education" by E. K. Townsend Coles. A paper written for an International Expert Panel on Adult Education and Development with Special Reference to the Arab States, 1975.

[8]See Manzoof Ahmed, *The Economics of Non-formal Education* (Praeger Publications), 1975. In the Foreword to this book, Charles S. Benson writes: "Ahmed presents evidence to show that the cost-savings of non-formal education reside mainly in reduced expenditures for human time. . . . But Ahmed warns us that costs of materials of instruction and equipment may be higher per enrollee in effective non-formal programmes than in formal programmes of comparable general quality. This is an important matter to recognise in designing non-formal programmes."

conviction that adults should pay for their education and that only in this way will the facilities offered be appreciated.

To these factors, two more need to be added. The first is that it is extremely difficult to calculate with any precision how much is spent on adult education. Many of the providing agencies seldom quote any figure for expenditure specifically on adult education. Take the case of Ministries of Health. No one would deny that the work of a village clinic has an educative side to it, yet the village health worker is probably not regarded as an adult educationist and her salary is certainly not recorded as being an expense to adult education. Equally it can be claimed that a proportion of the money spent on radio and TV programmes is going towards adult education. Whilst the overall amount allocated by governments to adult education continues usually to be far too small, it may well be larger than is sometimes recognized.

The second factor is this; how much money ought to be spent on adult education? What is the rationale for deciding the extent of the resources to be made available in a sector of education which is so all-embracing? These are questions which have to be answered by each government in the context of prevailing social, economic and political realities.

There are various formulae by which governments make allocations to the Ministry which is responsible for adult education. One way is to take the amount spent in the previous year, adding a small margin for expansion. Another is to set aside a fixed percentage of the total education budget for adult education; a third way is to base the allocation on an amount for each adult member of the population. It will be readily appreciated that in all these cases there has to be an arbitrary calculation at some point. Unlike child education where the results of altering financial inputs and constraints can be calculated with a fair degree of accuracy, adult education is a bundle of imponderables where the answers, in many cases, can only be reached by arbitrary decision. Ought more funds to be spent on one section of the community than the other? Are certain activities higher up the national priority list than others? How can the claims for the library service and cultural programmes be rationally determined? What allocation should be made for grants-in-aid to non-statutory organizations?

Aspects Which Can Be More Accurately Costed

Having raised these difficulties it must now be stated that there are some parts of the work for which the necessary financial provision can be gauged accurately. In the first place there is the basic structure which has been discussed in preceding sections of this chapter. The staff required at the national, intermediary and local levels can be readily converted into budget figures, as can also many of the proposed services such as training facilities and resource centres, and a fairly accurate estimate given for others such as the correspondence education unit. Since it is important that adult educationists are mobile it is essential to include a larger allocation for transportation than is the case for child educationists.

A more difficult estimate to make is the cost of what might be termed the regular programmes. Some idea will be known both of the needs and the likely capacity for activities at the various statutory centres, and from this an approximation of the expenses involved can be made. It will then be for the Treasury to decide what proportion of programme costs can be met from public funds.

Then there is campaign money; that is the funds which are required for special efforts whether they be of a few years duration as is generally the case with literacy, or shorter campaigns aimed at selected target groups or nationally to encourage thought about a particular topic. Examples of this might be campaigns related to health hazards, population education, or road safety. (All of these subjects should also have a continuing place in adult education programmes in addition to being chosen for special emphasis at a certain time.)

As with the regular programme, a fairly accurate estimate can be made of the cost of such operations.

This still leaves much that can only be gauged in some arbitrary fashion, though the final figure may not be reached in quite the haphazard manner which is sometimes envisaged.

Is Adult Education Education on the Cheap?

There is still only scanty information on which to base an answer to this question. Ahmed[9] cites two examples of expenditure which

---

[9]Manzoor Ahmed, *The Economics of Non-formal Education* (Praeger Publications, 1975), pp. 92 and 61.

provide contradictory evidence. Referring to a literacy programme in Tunisia he cites conclusions reached by Simmons that "the cost of the entire programme is the equivalent of $32.80 per student. Since, however, only 1 in 50 reaches the third year, and has then only a 70 per cent probability of obtaining simple literacy, the effective cost per simple literate is $1530. This is more costly than successfully bringing one primary student to the end of the fourth grade which is estimated in Tunisia at $600." On the other hand, Ahmed describes the school equivalency courses in Thailand, which are offered during the evenings with somewhat abridged syllabi and using the school staff and facilities. Students pay a fee that covers 78 per cent of the costs. Total costs per student of the course at three different levels with the equivalent cost per student in the formal system are as follows:

	Adult course	Normal school course
Level 3	627 bahts	1300-1800 bahts
Level 4	1372 bahts	3350 bahts
Level 5	1669 bahts	2200 bahts

These two examples serve to show that one ought not automatically to assume that adult education is an inexpensive activity. It may be more costly than is the case with formal education and certainly it requires considerable financial support.

How Can Costs Be Reduced?

There are several ways in which the cost of adult educational activities can be reduced. The greater reliance on the media and on volunteer staff; the development of self-instructional material; production of materials in quantity; and the combination of education with work for production are some of the ways in which the unit-cost of learning facilities for adults can be substantially brought down.[10]

---

[10]See P. H. Bertelsen, *The Economics of Adult Education* (Reader of Working Papers 1, International Expert Panel on Adult Education and Development with special reference to the Arab States, German Foundation for International Development, Bonn, 1975), p. 92.

Sources of Funds

Central government is the principal but not the sole source of funds. In many countries local government is also expected to allocate funds to adult education and there is too the contribution, in services and materials as much as in money, which voluntary community organizations make.

For some aspects of adult education and notably in vocational training, employers should be required to give financial support. This will be more readily done where the training is manifestly geared to the needs of industry and agriculture and where the employers have taken part in deciding the form and content of the activities offered. Once employers are assured that they will be consulted on matters of policy

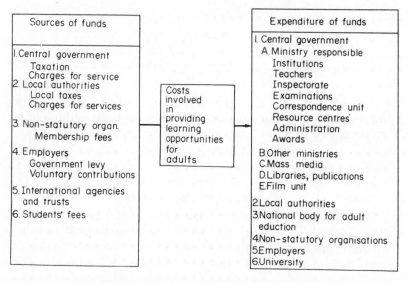

DIAGRAM 9. The sources of funds and those who spend
the money.

relating to vocational training it is reasonable to impose on them—with their willing consent if possible—a training levy, the money to be used exclusively for initial and in-service courses. The Reference Committee for Vocational Training mentioned earlier might well be renamed as the National Training Board, a title in use in several countries.

Some funds might also be obtained from international sources, either in the form of multilaterial or bilateral aid for specific projects or from charitable trusts.

Student Fees

The most contentious potential source of funds is that of the participants themselves. Is it essential that they should pay something or ought adult education be made a "right" as is increasingly the case with formal education?

The best answer probably lies in some sort of compromise. There are certain aspects of adult education which are aimed at specific target groups where payment of fees in money would be inappropriate. This is the case with most literacy programmes and extension work of the Ministries of Agriculture, Health and Labour. That is to say that where the activities are aimed at raising the economic potential and social wellbeing of those who can least afford to pay, the service should be without monetary charge. The participants may well wish, of their own, to make token payments in other ways such as hospitality and the construction of work benches. But the basic purpose of the programmes is to rid both the individuals concerned and the nation as a whole of a scourge, be it illiteracy, wasteful uneconomic farming, land erosion, or the dessimation of the population through disease and malnutrition. It would be ludicrous to put a price label on such activities.

There are, however, some aspects of adult education which ought to be priced. There are, for instance, those professional and vocational refresher and up-grading courses for the well-off where it would be wholly justified to charge an economic fee to the individual participants and paid for either by themselves or their employers. There are, too, aspects of general education, middle and upper level correspondence courses and some aspects of social and cultural education for which those benefiting ought to make some contribution to the costs.

It must be left to each country to decide which programmes should be free, which should be offered at a token fee to the individual and which should be self-supporting. This is a delicate task and one which the national body for adult education will need to review annually.

Attitude of Parents to Adult Education

In the developing countries the first thought of parents is for the education of their children. Where places are insufficient to provide every child with the opportunity of staying at school even throughout the primary stage, it is natural that every well-intentioned parent should not wish money to be diverted from the education of their children. It is highly likely, therefore, that any country intending to take adult education seriously must first conduct a public relations campaign to assure adults that money spent on their education is additional to the amount available for the formal education of children. The campaign would also have to make it clear why the government felt it essential to provide this form of education, indicating the ways in which better-educated parents can help their children improve their chances of success. As with all branches of adult education, it is essential for the providers to win and keep the confidence of the adult public they seek to serve.

CHAPTER 5

Teaching Methods, Aids and Buildings

Adult Learning

Any discussion on teaching methods should rightly commence with a consideration of the particular problems which adults face in the learning process and how best these can be overcome. This introduction will not attempt to discuss this complex subject in detail, since there is a considerable and growing literature on the subject.[1] Rather a selection will be made of the more important points which should be uppermost in the minds of adult educationists.

Many who have decided to take up studying do so with several disadvantages, the first being that they lack the confidence that they really can learn. There are then those who have had some previous contact with the formal education system and the experience is viewed with mixed feelings. "School" might well have been a dark, dank and dirty place and the information gained has not appeared, in later life, to have been particularly relevant. But perhaps the greatest hindrance to learning is that the materials and methods used in adult education are so often those of the school classroom and may well be inappropriate. The assumption is made that what was good enough for children will automatically be good for their parents. The adult is thus treated more as an overgrown child than a sensitive, mature individual. This comment applies especially to much literacy and general education teaching where many who volunteer to teach are primary school-teachers who find it difficult to adapt their methods when confronted with adults.

Most adults come voluntarily to learn. A sacrifice has been made to submit to such discipline, precious money and valuable time expended,

---

[1]A comprehensive book on the subject is *How Adults Learn* by J. R. Kidd (Association Press) New York, 1973.

and a deep-seated fear overcome. The attitude of most adult students will be one of expectation; they will demand that no time should be wasted, and they will certainly assume that visible results will be soon forthcoming from their labours. It will be important for the leader or animateur to retain this enthusiasm while at the same time getting the students accustomed to the idea that quick results are unlikely. Furthermore, the speed with which changes in attitude are promoted and new ideas accepted will vary with each person. For many, results will show only after hard and sustained work.

Experience of Life

Unlike a child, the adult brings to the learning process an experience of life. He will be conditioned by his own interests, prejudices and emotions as also by the attitudes of those around him. As an adult he may well have social responsibilities as husband and father, together with manifold community obligations. He will also be a breadwinner as employer, employee or what may be more likely as a self-employed person and the nature of his work may well constitute the major reason for his wishing to continue with his education. It is important for those who seek to help adults that they first try to understand the differing worlds in which they live and which exert such influence on them, though this is not easy since no two will have precisely the same background and store of experience. If the learning process is to be effective, however, it must be learner-centred and this implies that all experiences should be rooted in an understanding of the learner, and be so constructed as to keep him as the focal point. This is a marked distinction to those approaches whereby programmes are constructed either from presumed learner interests or from those of some other party, be that person a teacher, administrator or even a curriculum specialist.

The Paramount Rules of Learning

At the risk of over-simplification, the most important rule of learning can be stated simply as follows; the learner must derive satisfaction from the experience. This will be accomplished in a variety of ways. The work must be relevant, and what the learner feels in need of. Since most adult education is run on a voluntary basis, it is essential to retain the full interest of the learner, and this will only be possible where the content of the activity of whatever kind is meeting his requirements as he perceives them. The level of communication must be appropriate, and there must be the sense of security which is engendered by working from the known, the starting-point being the experience of the learner. Progression towards the unknown should be seen to be a gradual process, the new being used to reinforce what has gone before, since the ability to forget is an ever-present danger. Wherever possible relationships should be indicated between what is known, either from former discussions or through daily experience, and what is at present unknown. Clearly defined and reasonably attainable goals should be set, and at the conclusion of every session the learner should be stimulated by a sense of accomplishment that something new has been discovered. A sense of satisfaction will also be engendered where the learning process has been enjoyable. It is a sad reflection on educationists that learning is so often associated with boredom and dullness. For youths especially, but also for people of all ages, the act of learning should be made a thrilling and adventurous activity.

Programme Construction

The above comments should be borne in mind when programmes are being constructed, and when teachers and leaders are being trained for their tasks. A mark of the poor teacher is an inability to know how much new material or how many fresh concepts should be encompassed in any experience. Clearly no fixed rules can be laid down on this issue. The speed of advance of the learner will depend on many factors; the crucial point to be remembered is that it must be right for the learners in relation to the tasks being undertaken. Whilst too slow a tempo will breed boredom, too swift an approach leads to eventual confusion, frustration and loss of interest. Striking the right balance is an art which comes with experience; an awareness of the importance of doing so is the first step in gaining this skill.

Participation

The adult will respond best where he is encouraged to participate fully in the learning process. The report of the Second Unesco World Conference on Adult Education contains a paragraph on the "paramountcy of active methods"[2] and amplifies this by stating that "the aim is to instruct the adult with his own active participation". Two considerations arise from this dictum. The first is that participation should be encouraged whenever possible in the construction of activities being designed for adults. In those aspects of adult education concerned with attitude formation and inquiry into social, political, economic and cultural problems and issues, it should be regarded as an essential and indispensible first step that those involved should formulate what it is they intend to do. Some aspects of adult education, and especially those associated with the more formal learning programmes, do not lend themselves so readily to being participant designed; even so the scope of what it is proposed to do should be first explained and discussed and the reactions given due consideration.

The second point is that participation does not necessarily rule out such methods of teaching as lectures, but it does demand that in every learning situation there should be a two-way flow of communication. Closely allied to the need for learner-participation is the importance of variety. Boredom is an enemy of learning. Reinforcement of material in different ways enables new skills to be thoroughly learnt, without losing the essential interest of the learner.

Conduct of the Learning Experience

It is also important that the leader or teacher should avoid making detrimental remarks about the learner, either privately or in public. In a discussion, the member reluctant to speak may have adopted this guise through fear that others will laugh at his opinions. Inhibitions of this kind will only be broken down through the creation of confidence within the group that all views will be treated with respect; that when mistakes are made the learner will be helped to see what is wrong without ridicule. A word of encouragement will mean a great deal to an adult who possibly is deeply aware of his disabilities, real or presumed. The co-operative rather than the competitive spirit should be promoted. There should be no "marks" or "prizes". It is not impor-

[2]Report on the Second World Conference on Adult Education, *Educational Studies and Documents,* No. 46, Unesco, Paris, 1963, p. 16.

tant whether someone is learning more or less than another; the vital consideration is that all are learning as much as they can.

Physiological Decline

All adults suffer from physiological decline with age and several may also have been handicapped throughout their lives.[3] Special consideration, often requiring small but essential additional aids, must be exercised to enable those in particular need to benefit from the learning experience.

Decline with age is especially noticeable in countries where medical services are not universally available. Especial care must be taken with those who are handicapped through faulty sight or hearing. In a group they should be positioned advantageously to minimize the effect of their disabilities. Clear and audible speech should be used by leaders; teaching aids should be of a kind so that those with imperfect sight—a larger group than is often supposed—can still benefit from them.

Formal, Informal and Incidental

There was a period when adult educationists prided themselves as being the principal purveyors of informal education. At that time a distinction was drawn between formal methods, which implied a more disciplined approach to learning through a "teacher" and "taught" arrangement, and informal education by which a flexible, less structured experience was indicated. It is, of course, quite usual for the two to be mixed; that a formal class might, at a certain point, change approach and become informal. Equally so it is often desirable for an informal discussion to be opened in a somewhat more formal manner with a set talk.

At this time, too, the use of the term "incidental learning" came into the lexicon to refer to those chance, often unpremeditated, unconscious moments when learning took place in the life of an individual. From birth to death each time a person perceives the world around him there is the possibility of learning something new; the un-

---

[3]Unesco estimates suggest that one in seven people suffer from some kind of handicap.

expected encounter on the pavement; observing something different about the colour of leaves after a storm; grappling with the letters on an advertisement and eventually making sense of them; reading a newspaper. All of these experiences are subsumed under the title of incidental learning. Public authorities and others who are responsible for the environment should remember that this form of learning is a very potent force and is happening all the time. Every care should be taken, therefore, to set the highest standards possible in design of all kinds, since this is bound to have a beneficial effect on the level of cultural and aesthetic appreciation of the public as a whole.

It is unfortunate that there is such confusion about many of the terms in current use. As Coombs rightly remarks, "there is not yet a clear and commonly accepted terminology for discussing some of the important modes of education. . . .There is evident need for a new vocabulary appropriate to this field, but this will take time to evolve."[4]

In Chapter 1 there was discussion on the meaning of the terms adult and non-formal education as used in this book. From time to time there has been mention of the formal system of education referring to those activities which take place in primary, secondary and tertiary level institutions for full-time and registered participants. In this chapter when the terms formal and informal are used in the context of teaching methods, they refer to the situations described at the outset of this section. Incidental education is the one term over which there appears still to be no confusion and retains the meaning described above.

Learning Situations

An inventory of learning situations adopted for adult education would include the following:

    (i)   Those associated with single learners
       (a)   Individual tuition
       (b)   Correspondence tuition
    (ii) Those associated with a class or group

---

[4]P. H. Coombs, *New Paths to Learning,* International Council for Educational Development, New York, 1973, p. 10.

    (a)   Class or Group Learning under Supervision
       (1) Formal situations
       (2) Practical work
       (3) Demonstrations
       (4) Study visits
       (5) Projects
       (6) Role playing
       (7) Performances
    (b)   Class or Group Learning Unsupervised (often called study groups)
  (iii) Those associated with a mass audience
    (a)   Radio
    (b)   Television
    (c)   Campaigns

Tabulated like this might give the impression that each situation is wholly separate from the others. This, of course, is not so; and later in this chapter there will be discussion on the importance of combining various situations and methods in order to achieve maximum effect.

Importance of Relating Method to the Ability of the Teacher

Before considering these situations individually there are two important warnings to be voiced. First adult educational activities are often under the control or supervision of people whose capacity to teach adults is, for one reason or another, somewhat limited. At the basic level, much literacy work is undertaken by school teachers who are themselves not very proficient at their primary task. Many find it difficult to make the necessary adjustments when confronted by adults and fall back on the well-tried chalk-and-talk, dictatorial methods which inhibit learning in children and whose deficiencies are simply compounded when applied to adults. There are, too, the willing volunteers, at all levels of educational attainment, who assist in a wide variety of adult educational activities. These people tend to want to conduct meetings in the way they were treated at school. This is, after all, the only yardstick, the sole example to which they can refer, and in most cases the result is the same as with the "trained" schoolteacher.

There is one lesson which arises from these comments; since most part-time teachers will for various reasons lack expertise in teaching adults, it is essential that the methods and systems of teaching which are adopted are within their competence. It has to be remembered that the more informal and unstructured a method becomes the harder it is for the untrained amateur. This is not to suggest that the sterile ways of old should be resorted to but to emphasize the need of keeping methods as straightforward as possible, giving clear indications in teachers' manuals how to set about the work, and in training sessions concentrating on the bread-and-butter job of how to teach an adult.

Importance of Relating Method to the Social Customs of the People

The second caution is the necessity of ensuring that teaching methods do not offend the social customs of the people. It is not un-common for teachers and leaders in adult education to be working with people of a different tribe or community. Since the object of any activity is to help the people concerned and, as said previously, to be "student-centred", it is important that the teacher should under-stand the social milieu and pay careful account to local customs and attitudes. These could have a bearing on the teaching methods to be adopted, the protocol to be observed in conducting sessions, and the way in which the community as a whole can be involved without creat-ing resentment.

Furthermore, in most cultures there is a rich store of traditional forms of transmitting knowledge. These are likely to place strong emphasis on oral communication together with the use of dances, music and mime. The most successful learning activities are those which take place under conditions which are congenial to the learner; ways of acquiring knowledge through traditional procedures may thus prove to be the most efficacious.

Learning Situations Associated with Single Learners
Individual tuition

There are cases of people who enjoy learning entirely unaided, by themselves. The majority of lone learners, however, will respond to some assistance from a guide or tutor. The learner may be taking a course of instruction by correspondence, or be working for some professional qualification by himself. Whereas those studying at lower academic levels will receive help from other quarters—television, radio and study groups, all of which are considered later in this chapter—those who are working at a higher level may not get this kind of support because their numbers would not warrant provision of this kind. In the developing countries, however, such people constitute an invaluable potential human resource. At no cost to the taxpayer they are improving themselves and thus making an important contribution to the provision of the leadership on which development depends. Consequently they deserve whatever help can be given to them, a responsibility to which University Extension Departments in particular ought to be alive.

Tuition by correspondence

It may seem strange that this subject is being considered in the section on learning situations associated with single earners. Tuition by correspondence inevitably reaches out to a great number of people; in the majority of cases, however, the individual learners are perforce bound to do most of their studying by themselves.

Unfortunately, instruction by correspondence has been introduced into many countries under a cloud of suspicion. It has been described as the worst of all techniques of education. In the developing countries to argue about its merits and demerits is wasted effort. For many students it is likely to be a main channel open to them for advancement, and any discussion should concentrate on how to improve the effectiveness of the courses offered.[5]

Learning by correspondence is not easy, indeed most students find it difficult to discipline themselves sufficiently to keep at their work. Unless a fairly inflexible study schedule is adopted by each student it is easy to forget to do an assignment, and thus to fall increasingly behind until a position of hopeless despair is reached. Thus students studying by correspondence will need encouragement to stick to their work, and it is here that study groups and opportunities for occasional

[5]See Renée F. Erdos, *Teaching by Correspondence,* Longmans/Unesco, 1967, for a comprehensive account of correspondence teaching.

face-to-face tuition are so important. They will also need incentives, the most effective being that of financial reward. In some countries, for instance, students who complete all the exercises in a course are allowed to sit the examination for a reduced fee.

Since working by correspondence is essentially a solitary activity, it is essential that the material sent to students is clearly written and well produced. It should contain nothing which is not adequately explained, and for this reason it is best if it is conceived and produced in the country where it is to be used. Attempts at adapting material written for other countries is seldom successful unless the environment is broadly similar. The whole tone and language of the correspondence material must be right for the student.

Assignments must be carefully constructed as with other programmed material, and tested on small groups before being produced in quantity. Sometimes it is possible for assignments to include practical exercises. This is applicable not only for those courses which are related to academically oriented subjects but also for special courses which have been specifically designed for certain groups, often as part of their in-service training. For example, courses for agricultural extension officers designed to keep them up to date with new ideas might require them to perform certain functions whilst on their routine duties and record and report the results.

In some countries there may be a problem over which language to use in correspondence lessons. Whereas literacy material has to take account of local vernaculars this is generally not necessary or desirable with correspondence courses. Indeed the usual custom is for correspondence material to be written in the national language of the country, though exceptions to this may be made where there are large minority language groups.

Basic texts and a simple guide to study should be included in the material distributed with a course. Sometime it may even be necessary to arrange for the distribution of paper and writing books.

Long delay in the return of corrected correspondence papers is very discouraging to students. This is particularly the case where students have to send their written work abroad for marking, and reinforces the importance of each country running its own external studies department. But even where papers have only to travel short distances, delays due to poor postal services or faulty administration may occur and cause students to lose interest in their work. Indeed a prerequisite for a system of correspondence education is a reliable postal service or some other means of regular and speedy conveyance of scripts. Not only must written work be returned with expedition but the tutor's comments must be legible and helpful. Simply to mark an arithmetic sum as being wrong is not going to show a student working by himself how to put it right. It is also useful to include in assignments self-marking exercises and sample answers.

Correspondence courses are most effective when combined with other forms of instruction, a matter to be considered later in this chapter. This, however, greatly strengthens the case for governments to take over responsibility for general correspondence courses. In this way a close relationship can be formed between the controllers of the media and those concerned with preparing the written assignments. An example of how a correspondence unit works is given in Diagram 10 of the Mauritius College of the Air.

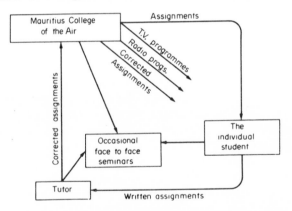

DIAGRAM 10. The relationship between a correspondence college and its students (from T. Dodds, The Mauritius College of the Air, *Journal of Mauritius Education*, No. 4, June 1975, p.54).

Learning Situations Associated with a Class or Group
Class or group learning under supervision: formal situations

Class or group learning under the guidance of a teacher or leader is the usual learning situation and the one regarded as most proper by many adults since it is most closely akin to the procedures of the school classroom. Where it is possible to provide a teacher or leader, and whether the situation is a formal one in which the "teacher" confronts a "class" of adult students, or the more informal procedures of group discussion under a leader are adopted, it is essential that the atmosphere should be one of enjoyment which springs from co-operative effort culminating in a sense of achievement. In both cases, the formal and the informal, it is so easy for the teacher or leader to give too much attention to the brighter members of the group and forget those who are facing real difficulties in their learning. A group may simply become a dialogue between a garrulous member and the leader, or worse still, a monologue from one or the other. The trained teacher of adults learns the art of bringing all into the learning process without making a public exhibition of the less-gifted, and of knowing how much or how little to contribute himself. These are skills which can be learnt, and which are further refined through experience. Since many teachers have had little or no training, however, nor are naturally endowed with such skills, it should not be too readily assumed that face-to-face teaching is the best method of instruction. Indeed, it is not unknown for the main obstacle to learning to be a poor teacher; thus emphasizing the importance of concentrating in training courses on teaching skills.

In learning situations of the kind being described, care must be taken with the physical layout. There was a time when the only arrangement was one of a teacher facing a class. As ideas of informality crept into the teaching armoury, so the desirability was advocated of changing the arrangement to one in which the leader and group were placed in a circle or semicircle and it was not long before this more informal arrangement was being used indescriminately for all occasions; reverting to the former was dubbed as being old-fashioned. Gradually, however, it has been recognized that the essential thing is to provide the right setting for the right experience. For example, if the emphasis in a particular session is on the use of pictorial aids, or writing on the blackboard it is manifestly better to have a seating arrangement in which all can see the things on display. On the other hand, where a group is meeting to discuss a problem, or to formulate a programme, the circular arrangement is likely to be more conducive to real discussion and interaction between members. One cautionary word, however; when adults are sitting opposite each other, it is best to give them a table on which to lean, or, as some might say, behind which to hide. An open, unprotected, circle may provoke embarrassment and fear rather than encourage participation on the part of the members.

Practical work

Much adult education is best taught through recourse to some form of practical work. Clearly this is the case with all vocational and domestic training but it is also true with many recreational and cultural pursuits. The apprentice will only learn how to use a lathe through constant practice on the machine. This must sound like a self-evident truism; it is surprising, however, how often it is forgotten, and even in vocational training institutions the percentage of time given over to practical rather than theoretical work is often much too small. There are, of course, reasons for this. Poor teachers may find it easier to put over the theory than supervise the practice; indifferently equipped workshops may be expected to accommodate too many students; impoverished administrations may have to economize on the materials available for teaching. However, it needs to be asserted with the utmost vigour that skills can only be successfully learnt where adequate time is given to practical work, and to economize on this, or to allow other teaching methods to reduce the time available for it, can have but one result; a reduction in the effectiveness of the training as a whole.

Of course, practical sessions often have to be combined with some theoretical teaching, and in designing workshops care should be taken to ensure that there is space for group work.

There are a number of ways in which practical skill training can be organized. In some subjects and particularly where the educational level of the students is broadly similar, it may be best to run the course on a group basis, that is, of all doing the same thing at the same time. In many cases, however, a system of free-pacing is better, and this is particularly so with short-term or accelerated training courses. Under these circumstances the students would have a number of practical exercises to do, graduated so that they become progressively more demanding. Each student would be free to move on to a fresh assignment once an exercise has been completed to the satisfaction of the teacher. The teacher would thus have to be available to give assistance to each individual student as necessary.

A particular form of practical skill training is that which associates the learning process with a commercial enterprise. A successful system of this kind is the Botswana Brigade movement.[6] A Brigade is formed only on local initiative, and where a community has expressed not just interest in the idea but also willingness to support the operation. Brigades are formed in any skill for which there is local demand. The trades most commonly learned are building, farming, dressmaking, motor mechanics, brick-making, pottery and crafts. Each year the intake into a Brigade is usually of the order of ten to fifteen, that is a group which can be supervised by one instructor. In essence the aim is to provide a member with up to 3 years training, the learning of the skill taking place mainly on the job. In return the student contributes through his or her work and production towards the wealth of the Brigade. This system has the advantage of not requiring large sums of money being injected into it since each Brigade is expected to generate its own resources through marketing its products, or selling the manual skills being learnt. It would give a false impression to suggest that the Botswana Brigade system has developed without difficulties. Not every Brigade has been successful and the system must still be regarded as experimental, even though it is now some 9 years since the first one was established. Nevertheless, as a means of spreading skill training at small financial outlay, it is clearly a model worthy of close examination.

Demonstrations

It is not always possible to arrange for every member of a group to perform a particular skill which is being learnt. There are also occasions when it is necessary to call people together to witness an operation being demonstrated.

The demonstration method of transmitting ideas and skills is a valuable additional learning situation, but one which obviously

---

[6]A full account of the Brigades is given in *Report from Swaneng Hill* by Patrick van Rensburg, the author of the movement. Published by the Dag Hammaskjöld Foundation, Uppsala, 1974.

demands the most careful preparation. Care must be taken to ensure that all those participating can really see what is being demonstrated and can hear any verbal commentary which is made. Before the demonstration commences there should be an introductory session to brief the participants on what they are going to see. Equally essential is time immediately after a demonstration for questions and discussion, ensuring that the message of the demonstration has been properly comprehended. Supporting literature is often a valuable further follow-up though this must be produced at a level which is appropriate to the learners.

Study visits

A study visit can be an interesting way of reinforcing things which perforce have had to be learnt in a more formal group situation. Environmental problems, for instance, which have been under discussion can be made more real by visiting areas which illustrate points which have been raised.

Projects

Projects, undertaken individually or in small groups, combine the learning of theory with practice. By enabling people to tackle problems and to seek to find solutions, this method of learning has a value far beyond the significance of the actual material being assembled and the knowledge gained. The project method has rightly found favour in the more progressive schools for children as also in adult education.

Projects must be challenging but, at the same time, within the reasonable grasp of the participants. Work done in small groups has the advantage over assignments given to individuals since this enables there to be interplay and discussion during the carrying out of the project; it also encourages the diffident and anxious, by giving them the support of colleagues.

Role playing

In this form of learning individuals or small groups enact situations, usually in a spontaneous manner. The presentation is then discussed by the group as a whole. This is a particularly useful device to bring out issues in a problem which is under discussion. It is important that as far as possible those actually performing should have volunteered to do so; care, too, must be exercised to ensure that comment is objective and not directed at personal shortcomings.

Performances

The value of using drama and dancing to illustrate and reinforce new ideas has long been recognized. In many developing countries there is a great wealth of natural talent in these arts which should not be wasted.

Unsupervised class or group learning

Where a teacher or leader is not available people may come together through what, in some countries, are known as study groups, that is, groups of adults who are studying a subject or considering a particular problem and who meet together, perhaps once a week or a fortnight, for mutual assistance. These groups are usually associated with courses of study in general education. What has been a problem to one may have been self-evident to another; the act of explanation can help both the recipient and the giver, who undergoes a form of revision.

The members of study groups may constitute most of the students in a district who are studying by correspondence. Since the formation of a group is likely to enhance the value of the tuition being provided, it should be considered whether its members might not receive some collective rebate on their course fees, the funds saved going towards the purchase of equipment for the group such as a radio, or for bursaries.

Study groups require organization, otherwise little work may be done. Fees have to be collected; a suitable meeting-place has to be found; a radio or television set, possibly on loan, has to be properly maintained. All these routine chores should be shared. Student study associations should be encouraged to administer the various study groups at different levels which are meeting in a village, community or district. Such associations would provide a channel for feed-back between students and the promoters of courses and programmes.

From time to time it may be possible to provide some tuition for study groups or, alternatively, members of study groups may be given the opportunity of attending short concentrated "schools", where salient features in a course of study are discussed and areas of particular difficulty explained. Such gatherings have a tremendous effect on the morale of students studying in unsupervised groups or by correspondence.

Learning Associated with Mass Audiences

Radio

The radio is the most potent method of mass education which is at present available, and it is surprising that there are still countries where it is being largely neglected for educational purposes. It is relatively inexpensive; receivers are cheap and are readily portable, the principle difficulties being the necessity of ensuring that batteries are available.

Programmes may be beamed at the public as a whole, or at specific vocational, social and interest groups.

Informally radio is used to appraise the public of current events through news broadcasts, commentaries and programmes of serious intent, albeit produced in a manner likely to evoke an interest in the widest possible audience.

Such programmes are a means of placing before the adult public issues of domestic and international concern and of encouraging frank discussion on such matters. Equally important is the stimulation of interest in cultural pursuits, and in the physical and natural heritage of the country. The programmes are enhanced if those responsible for libraries, galleries and museums are called in to assist in their preparation. These less formal programmes will be of particular encouragement to those in isolated positions who are in danger of becoming intellectually arid. Sometime each week should be devoted to talking about books, though such programmes breed frustration unless libraries and book-sellers are given sufficient time to see that the literature discussed is available.

Since the continuing education of the public is essential in any plan of national development, time should be allocated on radio for giving information about the educational provision which is available for men and women. Activities sometimes go unheeded simply because the potential students were unaware of their existence. A regular weekly programme announcing events and opportunities for learning would help to ensure that people know what is open to them. Such broadcasts have a further value; by referring to specific activities taking place they help to encourage a desire in others to learn and give added impetus to the efforts being made in adult education.

There are then broadcasts aimed at specific target groups. In countries where farming is the main means of livelihood, the importance of a regular radio programme of instruction, advice, news and encouragement for farmers needs no stressing. Where schools are staffed by inadequately trained teachers, regular broadcasts in which curriculum problems are discussed can be a means whereby the quality of the instruction given to children and to adults is raised. The value of such transmissions is greatly enhanced if the listeners can meet together in groups so that discussion can follow, and questions and points of particular interest fed back to the broadcasters and raised in subsequent programmes. Supporting literature will also add to the value derived from the broadcast and the associated discussion. The formation of radio listening groups has been shown to be a way of enhancing the effectiveness of radio programmes.

Women constitute the largest target group in the community and the value of regular broadcasts on matters specifically of interest to them is widely recognized. These transmissions, dealing with a range of domestic subjects including child-care, simple health topics, nutrition and other family issues are often used by women's clubs as part of their programme. It is natural that home-centred topics should predominate but this should not be to the complete exclusion of other subjects. Women are not just home-makers; they have interests and responsibilities as wide-ranging and as nationally important as men, and matters of political and social significance should also be represented in the programmes.

Rural dwellers constitute the majority of the population in most developing countries. Those living in the growing urban sprawls which sadly are a manifestation of modern development nevertheless constitute a large minority. Their problems and interests will be different in many respects from their rural countrymen, and these should also be reflected in appropriate radio programmes.

Television

Television has a more restricted usefulness than radio at present, but clearly the areas covered by this medium will increase annually, especially with the growing use of satellite communication. It is a particularly valuable aid for teaching reading and writing to illiterate people. Experience, supported by experimentation, suggests, however, that television lessons are more effective where the studio teacher is supported by a group leader or classroom teacher, and where viewing is thus in groups rather than individually.[7]

Timing of radio and television programmes

With both media care has to be taken to ensure that transmissions go out when adults are free to listen and watch. This usually means evenings and weekends for men; mornings and afternoons are also possible for some women. Since poor lighting is a common feature in rural life and not unknown, either, in the towns and cities, weekends are often the times of maximum usefulness. This may well cause a clash to arise between educationists and those concerned solely with entertainment, a matter which usually has to be resolved by legislative action.

Link between presenters and audience

Radio and television programmes can suffer from a failure on the part of those presenting the material to become identified with those for whom the programme is intended. Earlier in this chapter it was urged that teachers or leaders must know the people they are seeking to serve if their work is to be fully effective. This applies with equal force to those who communicate through the media. Not only must the language and format of the presentation be right for those for whom it is intended, but every opportunity should be taken to encourage feed-back from the audience through question and answer sessions, and by close contact with listening and viewing groups where these have been formed.

---

[7]K.K.R. Cipwell, "Teaching Adults by Television", *Faculty of Education Occasional Paper* No. 6, University of Rhodesia, 1966, p. 84.

Campaigns[8]

A method being increasingly employed when the aim is to encourage thought on specific issues or to put over a particular range of information to a mass audience is through national or regional campaigns. Campaigns are usually of fairly short duration, spanning possibly no more than a few weeks. They require the most careful preparation including the pre-testing of the material to be used on experimental groups to ensure that faulty and unclear elements are corrected before the campaign general begins. Advance publicity of a campaign should be given to whet the public appetite of what is to follow.

Campaigns are models of combined operations in two senses. First because they may well involve the whole armoury of teaching methods and situations, including the fullest use of the media. Secondly, campaigns will be of concern to the whole panoply of providing agencies, statutory and non-statutory.

A recent example was the "People and the Plan" campaign in Botswana,[9] co-ordinated and supervised by the University Department of Extra-Mural Services. In this case the purpose was to publicize, in language which could be readily understood by the people as a whole, the aims and content of the current Five-Year Development Plan. In the process of so doing much interest was aroused in the concept of development as a whole and the place of the individual in the nation's plans for advancement. The campaign depended heavily on Radio Listening Groups, which over 10 weeks met weekly, listened to special radio programmes, studied literature which had been distributed in advance, and let their views be known through question and answer programmes which were also broadcast.

Aids to Learning

This examination of learning situations will be completed by con-

[8]The term campaign has been used for a long time associated with literacy work. This has had a usefulness in certain political situations but generally has given the erroneous view that literacy is something which can be eradicated swiftly. In this chapter "campaign" is used to describe short-term national efforts to encourage thought on specific problems or to put over a limited range of information.

[9]Mary Coleclough and David Crowley, *The People and the Plan,* Vol. I, University of Botswana, Lesotho and Swaziland, 1974.

sidering the aids which are available to the learner. No attempt will be made to go into details since there is a large literature on the subject and each category of aid deserves more exhaustive explanation than is possible in this book.

The teacher or leader

It is often forgotten that the teacher or leader of a group is usually the most prominent of all the aids to learning. He, or she, is looked at, listened to, emulated, liked, disliked, worshipped or mistrusted. To many he is the source of all knowledge and certainly is a decisive factor in the success or failure of a given learning experience. How often has a potentially good talk been spoilt by a poor presentation, or the constant intrusion of an annoying mannerism? This may seem a trifling point to some but from experience it can be asserted that the most defective aid may be the teacher himself.

The venue

The importance of getting the most advantageous physical layout for a group or class has already been mentioned. There is also the need to consider lighting and ventilation, and indeed the appearance of the vanue as a whole. It is a pity that schools, particularly in the developing countries, are usually collections of damp and dirty rooms, poorly lit and inadequately furnished for their primary purpose and quite inappropriate for use by adults. Where this is the only accommodation available, daytime gatherings in dry countries are often very much better conducted out of doors in the shade of a tree—even if this makes demands on the skill of the teacher or leader.

Non-electrical aids

There is a great variety of aids which are available, and most of these can be made quite easily locally. Since the most effective aids are usually the simplest and consequently the least prone to breakdown, these are the ones that should be stressed in training sessions. The following is a list of the ones which are in most general use:

Blackboard

Posters, charts and maps

Flip-charts, that is a succession of charts put together in order to tell a story or illustrate the development of an idea.

Flannelgraph, where letters or pictures with a roughened underside surface cling to a board covered with some rough textured cloth. A more sophisticated, and less common variant of this is the magnetic board, where the objects on display adhere to a metal board by the use of magnets.

Aids requiring electricity

In this category the list of possibilities seems to grow daily. Since, however, they all involve complicated machinery and a supply of electricity or batteries, the chance of breakdown is much greater than with the non-electrical aids. With the possible exception of radio, not too much reliance should be placed on them. It is essential that the teacher is thoroughly conversant with their use and that a check has been made in advance of a session that the equipment is in working order.

A short list of this category of aids would include:

Radio

Television and video tape recorders and tape

Cassette and tape recorders

Overhead projector

Slide and film-strip projector

Cinematograph

Films

These deserve especial mention since the film can play a most important role in arousing interest, especially amongst audiences which are not used to seeing moving pictures. When films are incorporated in a learning session, it is beneficial if the leader opens with a brief introduction, highlighting the points the group should note. After the film has been shown there should be a discussion when the same points can be reviewed, and if the film is of short duration it can then be shown for a second time.

The written word

Despite the advent of radio and television, the written word remains the most potent form of communication with literate people and indeed there is evidence to suggest that the wider use of the media will increase rather than diminish the demand for reading material. Books, magazines and newspapers are likely, therefore, to continue to be an essential vehicle for learning.

The developing countries are still having to rely heavily on the industrialized countries for the books which are read. Unesco figures for book production in 1971 shcwed that in Africa 25 titles per million inhabitants were published, in Asia 59, and in Latin America 77, whilst in Europe the figure was 509.

The fact that the developing countries will have to depend on outside sources for their books makes it likely that much of the reading material may be irrelevant and lack reader-appeal. Strenuous efforts are being made to correct this balance, especially through officially-backed Literature Bureaux, where local authors are assisted in the publication of their manuscripts.

Books have to be produced for different levels of readers. Those for people with only an elementary ability to read should be graded and, if possible, marked in some way to indicate the size of vocabulary used. This helps to ensure that readers can be advised to select works they can comprehend. The type to be used and the form of illustration is also important, and will vary according to the readership.

The library service

Even where there are books there is no guarantee that they will become available to the public other than to the fortunate few who live in the larger urban centres near public libraries. The distribution of reading material is a major problem which usually requires governmental initiative through the establishment of a distribution system of book-boxes, a student book service and, where communications permit, the use of mobile libraries. Through all the means of publicity available, information should be given about the books available and how to obtain them.

All this presupposes that there is a National Library Service, directed by trained librarians and supported in the smaller centres by people who have some knowledge of library procedures. The senior librarians, responsible for quite small collections of books, but nevertheless an essential link in the chain between the book-store and the reader, should be given a short introductory training course on cataloguing, ordering and book repairing.

Both the selection of books for the library service and providing readers with guidance as to which to read are crucial tasks. Administrative problems can usually be overcome given sufficient goodwill and resources; the provision of the right literature and providing assistance to aspiring readers are harder requirements to meet. University adult education departments can help by giving advice to those adults who are attending their activities. Adult education staff in general should try to keep abreast of what material is available, and especially for those who need guidance on what to study.

Newspapers

The most read of all written material are newspapers, and this is so even though the average circulation of the daily press is low in the developing countries. Unesco figures show that the countries of Africa have an average of 14 newspapers, Asia 63, Latin America 90, North America 232, and Europe 258.[10]

Whilst in many countries there is a commercial press providing reading for people with a good basic education, it is often necessary for the government to produce a subsidized newspaper, especially for distribution in rural areas, with articles written especially for the newly literate.

Communities can often be encouraged to compile their own local newspaper though this may not be for distribution since it is unlikely that a printing facility would be available, but to be affixed to a board in some central position or at the community meeting-place if one exists. Wall newspapers are a useful device for publicizing local events and giving new literates in the locality something topical and interesting to read. They do, however, require someone in the village to shoulder the responsibility of organizing the newspaper.

---

[10]A. A. M'Bow, "Unesco at the Service of Education in Africa", *Educafrica*, Vol. 1, No. 1, June 1974, p. 9.

Static displays

Somewhat akin to the wall newspaper is the static display, where a particular piece of information is put over through the medium of posters, diagrams, models and photographs, together with simply worded explanatory captions.

The Need for Combined Operations

There are two cogent reasons why learning experiences should be planned as far as possible to make use of a number of situations and methods, apart from the obvious one that variety helps to ward off boredom, an enemy of learning.

The first reason is that learning takes place more readily and effectively if a number of the human faculties are brought into action. For example, a method which depends solely on hearing is likely to be less effective than one which combines speech and hearing. From this principle has been constructed the well-known pyramid of learning, the base-line experience being the one which probably involves most senses (including sometimes even taste!). Diagram 11 shows this pyramid, and set against it are typical learning situations, with an inventory of the senses which are likely to be brought into use at that time.

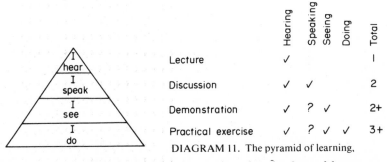

	Hearing	Speaking	Seeing	Doing	Total
Lecture	✓				1
Discussion	✓	✓			2
Demonstration	✓	?	✓		2+
Practical exercise	✓	?	✓	✓	3+

DIAGRAM 11. The pyramid of learning.

This is not to suggest that there is no place for the formal lecture or presentation; of course this is not so. But it does clearly point to the desirability of combining it with a discussion or project.

The second reason for advocating combining learning situations is that since one method reinforces the other, the maximum value will be derived from each. Uncoordinated, a system may fail; combined with others, and the process stands a better chance of achieving its objective. The most obvious example of this is correspondence education, which will be considered separately in the next section.

It is important, however, to consider carefully how these combinations are to be made. Take, for example, the use of radio. This medium is ideal for some aspects of adult education, but not suitable for others and too costly for a third category. Though radio lessons in theory can be compiled and broadcast for every level in the ladder of general education, in practice it is accepted that at the basic level of literacy radio is not a satisfactory medium, whilst those studying for external university degrees are likely to be too few to warrant the expense of special programmes. This suggests that radio should be used for programmes reaching out to a large audience, the main exceptions to this being in countries which have either very remote or nomadic communities which cannot be served in any other way.

It is wise for those controlling adult education to take careful account of the variety of methods and situations which are available and to ensure that the wisest combination is used in each circumstance. Table 5 gives an indication of the combinations which are applicable to some of the aspects of adult education which have been discussed in this and preceding chapters.

TABLE 5. *Teaching situations applicable for different levels and types of adult education*

	Class/group	Study groups	Individual tuition	Corresp. Educat.	Radio *	T. V. *	Press
General : Basic	✓					✓	✓
Middle levels	✓	✓		✓	✓	✓	✓
Upper	✓	✓	✓	✓			
Vocational training	✓			✓			
Civic/Social: Groups	✓	✓		✓	✓	✓	
Public as a whole	✓	✓			✓	✓	✓
Campaigns	✓	✓		✓	✓	✓	✓

* These columns refer to the use of the media as a vehicle for teaching and not as a means of arousing an interest amongst the public.

The Combination of Radio and Television
with Correspondence Courses

Correspondence courses are most effective when combined with some other form of instruction. Apart from direct teaching it is the media which complement correspondence tuition best. In most countries radio is much the more important since it is cheaper and usually has overall national coverage whereas television tends to be restricted to the urban areas.

Correspondence tuition, on the one hand, and radio and television on the other, should be regarded as complementary operations and not, as is so often the case, two separate entities which are then somewhat unhappily brought together. This implies that the designers of programmes and the writers of correspondence courses should work together. The time available for programmes is bound to be limited; certainly it is unlikely that there would be time for more than one weekly broadcast for each of the courses offered whether for in-service training or as part of a scheme of general education. It will only be practicable, therefore, for radio and television sessions to pick out the main points in a correspondence course concentrating on the likely areas of greatest difficulty. If it is possible for the transmissions to go out live rather than pre-recorded, the tutor could deal with specific problems which from student assignments and through other sources of feed-back have proved to be particularly difficult, or where the correspondence script has been shown to be faulty.

Once a correspondence course is rigidly tied to a radio or television programme it loses one of its outstanding advantages, namely its flexibility. Students ought to be able to commence a correspondence course at any time, and within limits, work at their own speed. If the broadcast lesson becomes essential listening the course loses these two virtues. Furthermore, it makes it impossible for those students who miss a transmission through illness or for some other reason, to catch up on the material lost. If repeats are possible so much the better but even so it is as well to conceive the broadcast material as a valuable aid to but not essential listening for correspondence courses, thus preserving the important element of free-pacing. At the same time the usefulness of combining correspondence tuition and radio and television programmes must be stressed to potential students, and every effort made to enable both forms of learning to be used to-gether.

Buildings and Other Capital Equipment

Use of existing facilities

Adult education is the least demanding of all branches of education for capital installations. Many activities take place in premises which were designed primarily for some other sector of education or community work. Thus a first task for those responsible for adult education is the compilation of an inventory of all the facilities which are available. This will include schools, colleges, halls, community and social centres, libraries and other public places. It would be folly to embark too hastily on a building programme until it is known precisely what is already available. Also it is criminal if public institutions such as schools are being under-utilized, often through lack of legislative sanction or because of some petty administrative hindrance. It is not unknown for a caretaker to be the sole obstacle preventing the use of a school for adult work in the evenings and at week-ends. It is essential, therefore, to ensure that the costly facilities available are fully used by being made freely available for adult groups. This, however, places a responsibility on those sponsoring activities in borrowed premises for the maintenance and security of the buildings and equipment.

Administrative premises

The requirements for adult education in this category are likely to be modest; they are none-the-less important, for without adequate office space, it would be impossible to administer an effective system. Rooms will be required within the Ministry responsible for adult education; some also will be needed at the intermediate levels of control in the provinces and districts.

Programme Buildings

Vocational training

The larger institutions for skill training, offering courses in the mechanical, electrical, building, commercial and other vocational skills, are usually controlled either by another branch of the Ministry of Education or by the Ministry of Labour. In both cases such institutions do not come within the responsibilities normally assigned to adult education. In countries where adequate facilities for skill training do not exist, however, it is often the duty of the adult educationist to be pressing the case for their establishment.

Rural skill training centres

The centres referred to in the preceding paragraph are usually to be found in urban areas. Increasingly, however, it is being recognized that there needs to be the complementary development of skill training centres in the rural areas, providing training in those crafts which are required in the locality at a level of technology which is appropriate to the people. Such centres ought not to be costly installations, and at best the communities to be served should be consulted on their siting and programme and be encouraged to assist with their construction. In the Sudan there are centres which consist of a classroom and an adjoining covered work area for crafts such as carpentry. The surrounding yard is used for brick-laying instruction. In Swaziland the centres being planned will also serve as depots for governmental extension services in agriculture and health, as well as being the local focus for other adult educational activities including literacy. Some of the centres will be associated with schools, care being exercised to ensure that the "adult" component is not delegated to being of secondary importance—a likely danger when a rural centre catering particularly for youths and adults is too closely linked to an institution of formal education.

Farm training centres

Related to the rural centres, but somewhat more costly, are the farm training centres. These institutions usually incorporate residential accommodation so that short intensive courses can be held. In addition to providing the venue for agricultural and domestic skill training for men and women, such centres are often available for other adult educational activities and may in fact also function as rural skill training centres.

Urban adult education centres

As a rule, adult educational activities of a general kind will take place in borrowed premises, and it is worth restating the principle that a country should make the fullest use of existing premises before embarking on a building programme. Sadly this sometimes results in adult education being treated as a second-class or fringe activity. However, as the significance of continuing education takes root there will be a corresponding move to make all educational buildings available for all sections of the community on an equal basis.

In the large urban complexes, however, there is usually a need for special adult centres so that educational activities for youths and adults can be organized throughout the day. Such places consist of meeting rooms, offices, a library and sometimes a refectory.

Neighbourhood centres

Where it is not possible to make use of schools or halls, it will be necessary to provide small centres in which adults living in noisy or overcrowded urban townships can study quietly and in light which is strong enough to permit of serious work without doing damage to the eyes. Centres of this kind often need to be no more than two small rooms; one a general reading room and the other furnished for group meetings. Centres may be financed by the community itself, by local government or by an industrial undertaking with plant in the locality. Somewhat akin to these centres are the Viewing Centres which are a feature of some countries where television has been introduced. According to climatic conditions these may be no more than covered areas with seating and a weatherproof construction for the receiver.

Polyvalent centres

A variant of the general adult education centre is what is known as a polyvalent centre, the prototype of which is in India. These centres provide facilities for all forms of activities, vocational, general, social and cultural, indeed very much what good adult education centres have been doing for a very long time. Polyvalent centres, however, are often connected with industrial undertakings, thus linking them closely with work-oriented activities.

Correspondence education

In countries where correspondence education is an important feature in adult education—and this is likely to be most developing countries— it is increasingly recognized that it ought not to be left to commercial operators concerned primarily with profit, but be provided either by the statutory authority responsible for adult education or by a parastatal body working under governmental sanction. This is to ensure the maintenance of high standards, co-operation with the authorities responsible for the media, and the introduction of correspondence teaching to all aspects of adult education and not only for general "second chance" programmes.

When correspondence education is regarded as a serious aspect of adult education it will be necessary to make provision for a national as well as for intermediate level distribution and collection points. National premises, as found in Kenya, Botswana, Mauritius and elsewhere, should include the space required for the quite considerable administration involved, an accounting department to deal with student fees, rooms for course writers and evaluators, and a recording studio for the production of casettes for use on radio and with tape recorders. There is then the production and mailing unit, needing more space than is usually allocated to it, as well as provision for the bulk storage of paper and stocks of course scripts. When designing buildings it is essential that the space is allocated in such a way as to facilitate the flow of material in a logical progression. Distribution and collection depots will be needed in the country, preferably located in institutions dealing with other aspects of adult education.

Libraries, museums and galleries

The necessity of establishing a library service has already been discussed. Though the need for a national museum and art gallery must perforce be regarded as of a lower priority to much other urgently needed requirements, it is nevertheless an important facility and one which should not be neglected. If possible small travelling exhibitions of national and foreign art should be arranged. This helps to develop a pride in the indigenous culture and an awareness of traditions from elsewhere. Exhibitions should also be arranged of local, national and foreign advances in science and technology, thereby stimulating public interest in the process of contemporary developments. Museums should be as interested with the affairs of today as of yesterday.

Community schools

The point was made earlier that the day will soon come when all educational institutions are designed to be open to all age-groups in the community. In the third world it is particularly important that this should be so in order that the fullest use is made of the capital being invested in their construction.

In many countries it is the primary school which is the first institution to be converted into a community facility, though secondary schools also are being designed and equipped for the same purpose. In Liberia primary schools are now being constructed with an annexe of one or two rooms for use throughout the day by adults, and the school as a whole is being regarded as the focal point for many community activities.

Residential colleges

Residential adult education colleges have been established in several countries to meet the need for accommodation which is solely for use by adults where courses, conferences, seminars and workshops can be held and at which the participants can both live and work together. Examples in Africa are Kivukoni College, Dar-es-Salaam, Ranche House College, Salisbury and the college at Tsito, Ghana. Residential colleges tend to vary greatly in character and purpose according to the motives of the founders; in the main they are controlled by independent boards, though they often have some connection with the statutory authorities or a parastatal body such as a university.

The three colleges quoted above illustrate the different functions which such places perform. Kivukoni grew out of the desire of members of the Tanganyika African National Union for a place which could help equip them for their responsibilities in the nation. The college thus emphasizes long-term training courses for potential leaders in the political life of Tanzania. Ranche House is an independent privately financed college. It is the venue for a variety of short courses and conferences, as well as being a local centre for non-residential adult education. Tsito came into being because the local community wanted a central meeting-place for educational activities sufficiently strongly that they translated their desire into reality by constructing the initial buildings themselves and by supporting the institution through contributions of money and in kind.

The value of having colleges specially for adults is that they are available at all times and whose staff are concerned solely with adult education.

Resource and Information Buildings

Training and resource centres

This is the most important of the buildings required specifically for adult education. A national Training and Resources Centre need not be an expensive building, though its cost is increased where it is decided to incorporate a book and materials production unit. This may be necessary in some countries, either because existing printing facilities are inadequate, or where the use of vernacular languages precludes the purchase of books from elsewhere. The training wing should contain residential accommodation for the students undergoing training in adult education, a subject discussed in the next chapter. Its size will depend on the needs of the country and whether other institutions, such as a univeristy, are providing courses in adult education. It may be concerned solely with short, intensive courses, or it may also have to be the venue for longer professional training courses for full-time workers, or a combination of both.

The Resource Centre should be linked to the Training Centre, containing a reference and documentation unit, space for the production of teaching aids and possibly facilities for film-making and a photographic workshop. The correspondence education unit and the offices of the rural newspaper would also be at the Centre.

Depending on the size of the country, sattelite centres may also be required at the intermediate levels. These would be the venue for short training courses, mainly for part-time teachers and leaders, though often these can be more economically conducted in borrowed premises. They would be the depots for the regional distribution of material and equipment of all kinds, including correspondence scripts, radios and batteries for listening groups, and books boxes distributed by the library service. A small equipment maintenance unit should be incorporated in each centre.

Both national and regional centres would be used by all agencies providing educational programmes for the community. They would be part of the Common Services which the Ministry responsible for adult education makes available to all providers.

Guidance centres and education shops

It is important to be giving people information about the activities which are available and of encouraging the idea that education is something interesting and valuable. To help ensure that people really do know what is on offer, guidance centres, or education shops, as they are sometimes called, should be developed, possibly associated with libraries or other public buildings.

Mobile facilities

In sparsely populated countries where buildings suitable for use by adults are not available it may be necessary for the statutory authorities to make vans available to take teams of two, three or more leaders to remote places to conduct seminars and short courses. These vehicles should be equipped to carry all the teaching equipment required and they may also provide accommodation for the staff.

Mobile libraries and cinemas—the two can be combined—are a means of ensuring that rural communities are not neglected and starved of adult educational activities. Maintaining such services, however, is costly and requires good administration; in the case of libraries, the regular delivery to villages of the less glamorous but possibly more reliable book-box by means of the local bus may, in the end, provide a better service to readers.

CHAPTER 6

Staff, Training, Research and Evaluation

Staff

The need for some full-time staff

With the possible exception of vocational training, all other departments of adult education have to function with a minimal full-time staff. It is still often the case that the person responsible for it at the Ministry of Education is so over-loaded with other duties that no more than a fraction of his time can, be devoted to adult education. That this situation is beginning to change makes it no less imperative to point out that a satisfactory system of adult education cannot operate without an adequate cadre of full-time, professionally trained, workers. No other branch of education tries to do so without this support; it is unrealistic and foolhardy to imagine that adult education can or should attempt to do so. Lowe rightly comments that "one of the main barriers to improving adult education programmes and to initiating new ones is the absence in most countries of a sizeable corps of highly-qualified, full-time professional staff. . . .The evidence is quite conclusive that no single factor is more conducive to the quickening of activity than the appointment of full-time staff!"[1]

Demands for full-time staff, however, have to be made with due regard to the availability of trained people, and the amount of money which a country is willing to allocate to adult education. The proposals which follow are made with one eye on economy; at the same time it should be recognized that a hopelessly inadequate establishment of full-time personnel probably results in a wastage of resources. Too few people, stretched beyond reasonable limits, usually means that practically nothing can be done; in short there must be a basic

[1] J. Lowe, *The Education of Adults: a World Perspective*, Unesco/OISE, 1975, p. 132.

minimum of staff for any worthwhile results to be achieved. This chapter will outline the essential staff needed for adult education.

Career structure

The position in most countries is that the career prospects for those wishing to work in adult education is far from satisfactory. There is a wide-spread feeling that if you want to get to the top of the educational profession as a whole, the only safe route is by working up through the formal system. Again, times no doubt are changing. If a country really wants to keep good people in adult education—and there is little point in spending money on training if they don't—then it must first dispel the notion that the big jobs are only for those who have climbed the conventional ladder. To achieve this it is essential to ensure that there is a continuum of appointments in adult education from the bottom to the top. A recognized career structure is thus all-important for the development of adult education.

The need for women on the staff

It is unfortunate that it is still necessary to have to remark on the necessity of ensuring that there are women on the staff of adult education departments. Clearly if women and girls are going to be encouraged to continue with their education, it is essential that this branch of education should be as much under the vigilance of women as of men.

Staff requirements in general

The two essential requirements for any system of adult education are first that there should be teachers or leaders available either directly to supervise group or class work or indirectly to instruct through correspondence courses and programmes on radio and television, and secondly an administrative structure which ensures that those who wish to learn and those able to teach are effectively brought in touch with each. The system thus requires administrators and teachers, one distinction between adult education and other branches of the profession being that of the full-time staff the former has a much higher proportion of administrators to teachers than is the case with the latter. This is because so much of the teaching provided for adults is undertaken by people working part-time at the job, and very often on a voluntary basis.

Table 6 indicates in general terms the staff needed for a system of

TABLE 6. *Staff requirements in adult education*

Level	Ministry responsible for A.E.	Other ministries	Non-statutory organ .
Village/ community	Leader (PT) Teachers (PT)	Visitors Extension workers	Voluntary helpers (PT)
Area	Area Adult Education Officer Teachers, Group Leaders (PT) Clerical Staff Maintenance Technician Driver/Mechanic	Area staff	Voluntary helpers (PT)
Province	Provincial Adult Education Officer Specialist Advisers Specialist Teachers Accounting and clerical staff Training and Resource Centre staff Maintenance Technician Driver/Mechanic	Provincial staff	Permanent staff of voluntary organ. University extension staff Educational staff of large industries, trade unions, co-operatives
National	Inspectorate Head of Department Departmental Staff: Administrative Accounting Clerical Examinations Board Mass Media Correspondence Unit Training and Resource Centre Library Service Specialists	National staff of operational Ministries Radio/T.V. Corp. Film/Cinema unit Printing press	Education staff in voluntary organ. Trade unions, co-operatives, large industries University Dept. of Adult Education

(PT)= part time.

adult education. It will be necessary to adapt it to meet the requirements of each country since obviously there will be variations according to needs and priorites and the availability of resources.

Since in most countries it is necessary to have intermediate levels between the "consumer" and the national headquarters, two such have been incorporated into this table.

The Village Leader or Development Agent

The linchpin in any system of adult education is the person who first effects the introduction between learner and teacher; who comes in contact with the individual seeking educational support and is able to advise him or her on what is available and how to set about obtaining help. Such a person can have a variety of titles amongst which are leader, development agent, animateur, facilitator, local adult education officer, and community development worker. The title is unimportant; for brevity the single word Leader will be used in this chapter.

A leader would be associated with small communities preferably of no more than 1500 inhabitants. In rural areas the person would probably be working in a cluster of villages or possibly a small town; in large towns, there should be a leader serving each community or neighbourhood. The village leader would be the *animateur,* the keen person with ideas and drive, seeking to ensure that the educational needs of adults are met, helping with the organization of local activities, distributing material and possibly undertaking some of the teaching. The leader would be in close touch with the part-time teachers and helpers living in the locality. Equally important is the relationship upwards, since the leader would be the link with those in authority at the higher levels.

When described in this way the duties of leader appears so complex as to warrant a full-time appointment. An enthusiastic person could, however, undertake this work part-time, and indeed this is generally necessary since it is unlikely there would be funds to pay leaders anything more than a token honorarium. Many leaders will, in fact, be people already employed by the government in either teaching or local administration.

Leaders should work closely with other community workers such as health visitors, agricultural and community development extension workers and youth leaders. Indeed, in view of the relationship which exists between the work each is undertaking, it might be deemed best to combine the administrative and organizing duties of all these and assign them to a local development agent, leaving the actual technical work to be provided by visiting specialist representatives from each of the agencies. Such an arrangement raises obvious administrative problems, since it would have to be decided to which Ministry the agent would be ultimately responsible, and a clear directive given to other ministries to work through the one person; there are, however, positive gains, since at the village level it is unrealistic to keep activities strictly in separate ministerial pidgeon-holes, and it is much better to be viewing the development process as a whole.

The Ministry Responsible for Adult Education

Area Staff

Leaders will need supervision; if allowed to work in isolation they may become disillusioned and frustrated. To help guard against this it is suggested that villages and towns should be grouped together into Areas, the size of which will vary according to needs and resources available. If possible areas should be delimited according to local government boundaries since this obviates any confusion which might arise as a result of there being more than one system of demarcation. The Area is also the distribution point for material and equipment supplied from the national headquarters for use in towns and villages. It is thus at the fulcrum between provider and consumer and it is essential that at this level there should be a person working full-time in adult education. A designation for this appointment could be Area Adult Education Officer (AAEO).

The AAEO would be responsible for the whole development of adult education in the Area, finding and registering local people willing to serve as part-time or voluntary teachers—an important task especially in places where many literacy groups are being formed—making arrangements for suitable venues to be available, distributing material to leaders, and undertaking general administrative supervision. He or she may have to organize short training sessions for leaders and part-time teachers, though in this work the assistance of specialist staff may be called upon. Finally the AAEO should be in close contact with representatives of all the other statutory and the non-statutory agencies operating in the locality, seeking wherever possible to promote an atmosphere of co-operation nurtured by acts of mutual assistance.

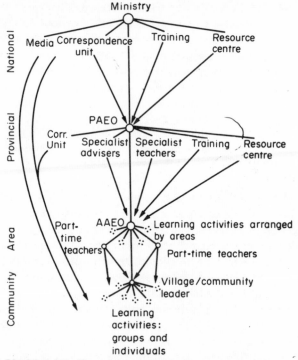

DIAGRAM 12. The provision of adult education by the Ministry
which has overall responsibility for it.

For this work to be satisfactorily accomplished, the AAEO will require
clerical assistance, a driver/mechanic and if great reliance is being
placed on the use of radios and other equipment a maintenance technician. Obviously a suitable vehicle must be at the disposal of the
AAEO.

Provincial staff

There may be several stages between the Area and the national staff
at the Ministry. For convenience only one is described in this chapter,
designated as the Province. The Provincial Adult Education Office
(PAEO) will be responsible for a group of areas; he or she will be the
principal agent of the Ministry in the field, concerned with implement-
ing national policy and adapting it, where necessary, to the special
requirements of the locality.

According to the particular needs of the province the PAEO will require the assistance of specialist advisers in aspects of adult education. The most obvious example is likely to be that of literacy; another might be for the encouragement of co-operatives, where these feature prominently in development programmes, and a third for the expansion and strengthening of activities for women. The advisers will be available to go out into areas and communities as required; another of their tasks will be instructing at provincial staff training courses. The province will be in the distribution point to the Areas for all kinds of teaching material produced in the national resource centre, and it may well be the posting and collecting point of correspondence scripts.

In all probability it will be at the provincial level that there is need also for specialist teachers, especially in vocational subjects associated with technical institutions. At times these teachers or instructors may work from mobile units, visiting small towns and village clusters, rather than exclusively in the central institution. This will make it possible for quite small communities to be given some skill training without the necessity of having to provide boarding accommodation for the participants. Examples of this would be in such practical crafts as carpentry, masonry and elementary motor mechanics; in such circumstances one or two instructors might remain in a village for a month or so.

Though technically on the national staff, it is probable that members of the Inspectorate will be based at Provincial headquarters - possibly one Inspector to each Province.

Sufficient clerical, accounting and maintenance staff will be required, as also are drivers for the mobile units. If it is decided to make the Province rather than the Area the centre for equipment repairs and supplies, a maintenance technician will be needed.

National staff

The need for a properly staffed national department has already been advocated in Chapter 4. Without this it will not be possible to develop a comprehensive and effective system of adult education.

In Chapter 4 the range of professional staff required at the national level was indicated. At first sight this may seem a formidable army of people, especially when compared with the way in which some countries presently organize their adult and non-formal education. The assumption is made, however, that a country embarking upon the provision of a system of adult education will wish it to be as effective as other branches of education. If this is the case it will be readily seen that the proposed divisions have their near counterparts in the formal system, and that nothing more is being asked for adult education than is provided for primary, secondary and tertiary education, as Table 7 illustrates:

TABLE 7. *Comparison between the ministerial requirements for adult education and other branches of education. The numbered divisions are those mentioned in Chapter 4, p. 77*

Primary	Secondary	Tertiary	Adult (non-formal)
1. Admin/Finance	Admin/Finance	Admin/Finance	Admin/Finance
2. Inspectorate	Inspectorate	—	Inspectorate
3. Teach.Trng.Coll.	Univ.Dept.ofEdn.	Univ.Dept.of Edn.	Training Centre
4. Teacher Centres	Teacher Centres	Univ.Inst.of Edn.	Resource Centres
5. —	—	Univ. Inst. of Edn.	Evaluation Unit (in Univ.Inst. of Edn.)
6. Exam Board	Exam Board	Exam Board	Exam Board
7. Libraries	Libraries	Univ. Library	Library Service
8. —	—	Open University	Correspondence Unit
9. Schools' Radio/TV	Schools' Radio/TV	Open University	Mass Media
10. — —.	Subject Committees	Faculties	Reference Committees

At the same time it has to be recognized that a country newly establishing its system of adult education will not be in a position to staff all the divisions suggested immediately, or to make adequate provision in every particular simultaneously. Suitable people will have to be found and trained for the work and it will take time to do this; there will also have to be a phased increase in financial allocation to adult education. It is likely, therefore, that initially some divisions may have to be doubled-up, and the staff appointed undertake a number of duties. A hypothetical three-phase development of a national department for adult education is shown in Table 8.

TABLE 8.   *A hypothetical three-phase development of a Department of Adult Education in the Ministry*

Phase I	Phase II	Phase III

1. Admin/Finance
2. Exam. Board
   Inspectorate
	1. Admin/Finance
	2. Exam. Board
	   Inspectorate
		1. Admin/Finance
		2. Exam. Board
		
		3. Inspectorate

3. Mass Media
   Correspondence
 	
4. Training
   Resources
   Evaluation
   Reference
   Libraries
	3. Mass Media
	   Correspondence
	
	4. Training
	   Evaluation
	   Reference
	
	5. Resources
	6. Libraries
		4. Mass Media
		
		5. Correspondence
		6. Training
		7. Evaluation
		8. Reference
		9. Resources
		
		10. Libraries

N.B.   The divisions *below* the line tend to be common services provided by the Ministry and available to be used by all the providing agencies.

The number of staff required in each division will vary from one country to another, according to the demands made on each and the degree of priority given to them. In some countries, particular aspects of adult education may warrant divisions of their own. The three most likely areas are Literacy, Vocational Training (especially where the entire responsibility for this rests with the Ministry of Education) and General, Cultural and Social adult education. Where this is the case the Reference Committees would be up-graded to the status of Divisions.

By far the most important staff appointment is that of the person to head up the whole enterprise. It will be desirable, if possible, to find a person who has had professional training in adult education. Unfortunately, in the present state of affairs this is likely only in a minority of cases.

Also of crucial importance is the recruitment of the right people to the Inspectorate, since the maintenance of good standards of teaching and administraion are essential.

The Army of Teachers, Group Leaders and Instructors Required

This section could not be started more cogently than by quoting from an address of Julius K. Nyerere, President of the United Republic of Tanzania. "But as well as being student, we all have to be willing to be teachers. We have to be willing to teach whatever skills we have by whatever methods we can—by demonstration and example, by discussion, by answering questions, or by formal classroom work. If we all play our part, both as students and teachers, we shall really make some progress. I would like to remind you of the promise of TANU (Tanganyika African National Union) members, I shall educate myself to the best of my ability and use my education for the benefit of all."[2]

The emphasis so far has been on the provision of the necessary administrative and specialist personnel needed for adult education. Some brief mention has been made of the teachers required but it is now time to redress the balance and give due emphasis to those who must be regarded as the vital front-line troops in adult education. An army must have generals, heavy artillery, and many ancilliary services; even in modern warfare, however, there is always the crucial need for the infantry.

Teaching and instructing adults will be undertaken by some full-time staff and many part-timers, the majority of whom will be volunteers for the work; of the full-time personnel, the most prominent will be specialist teachers in vocational subjects, extension workers in agriculture and health, university extra-mural staff, and full-time personnel employed by industries, trade unions and co-operatives for educational duties.

Most teaching, however, will be provided by those offering their skills on a part-time basis, and to find such people is one of the primary tasks falling to PAEO's AAEO's and Leaders. Some countries have devised schemes of national service teaching, using young people as volunteer teachers working for small wages instead of having to serve in the armed forces. Other countries, such as Cuba, Ethiopia and Somalia, have required secondary school pupils to assist in campaigns, especially for the teaching of illiterates. Everywhere, however, there is likely to be more work to be done than there are people available to

[2]Quoted in *Adult Education and National Development,* Directorate of Adult Education, Government of India, New Delhi, 1974, p. 29.

do it, and it will be necessary, by all the means of encouragement, to persuade volunteers to come forward and offer their services as part-time teachers; and this will require some effort since many will be diffident to take on tasks to which they are unaccustomed.

An important distinction between formal and non-formal education is that whereas the former tends only to use school teachers the latter makes full use of the total human resources which are available. Teachers will certainly be called upon, as is discussed in a moment, but so too will doctors, peasant farmers, housewives, bank managers, store-keepers and priests; anyone with a skill which is needed by someone else.

In many communities, great reliance will be placed on those already in the teaching profession to undertake part-time work with adults. The final report of the 1965 Teheran Conference on Adult Literacy comments that "it would seem only natural to call upon school teachers, at any rate as a transitory measure or on a part-time basis, although in certain cases this may impose a heavy burden on teachers who already have more than enough to do in the schools".[3] Increasingly as schools are seen to be institutions for the community as a whole, and not just for a limited age range, the full-time teaching staff will be expected and required to devote some of their time to the

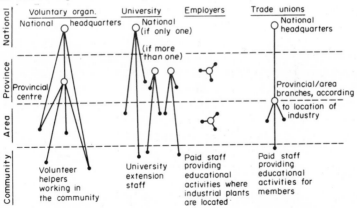

DIAGRAM 13. The non-statutory provision of adult education.

[3] World Conference of Ministry of Education on the Eradication of Illiteracy Final Report, Unesco, 1965, p. 37.

adult public, though to do this work successfully will necessitate training in suitable teaching methods.[4]

There is the question whether voluntary and part-time staff should be paid or whether the contribution they make should be regarded as an unpaid act of service to the community. They have skills and knowledge which others lack; should they be willing to give of their time in helping those less fortunate, or is some kind of remuneration desirable?

It would be unwise to be dogmatic on this issue; much excellent work is being done voluntarily, and the spirit of self-help is one to be supported. In many communities there are not the resources available to make it possible to pay teachers. Voluntary organizations have depended very largely on unpaid service, and this has been an important factor in stimulating a sense of responsibility one for another. Voluntary unpaid work can be as good and consistent as any other; the fact that a person is paid for working does not necessarily mean that it will be done better than those who give their services. At the basic level of literacy teaching there will have to be in any case great dependence on unpaid teachers.

At the same time, where the services of a part-time teacher or helper are frequently required, a strong case can be made for offering some remuneration. It is not only reasonable that this should be done; it also affords some measure of insurance to the students. It is notoriously difficult to maintain standards with unpaid helpers. The acceptance of remuneration, however small, places an obligation on the recipient and makes it easier for inefficient or unsufficiently equipped teachers to be replaced. Payment to part-time teachers, as to full-time staff, should be according to nationally recognized scales. Those part-time teachers who wish to do so can always donate their fees to good causes should they prefer not to keep the funds themselves.

The Training of Staff

Essential attributes of the teacher

For the teacher or instructor of adults, the first requirement is that he or she should be sufficiently qualified in the subject or subjects

---

[4]For a full discussion on the use of teachers in adult education reference should be made to *The Role of Teachers in Out-of-school Education;* Report of an Asian Regional Meeting, Unesco, Bangkok, 1974.

taught. This does not mean that the teacher has to be a specialist; there is always an abundance of openings for those with lowly qualifications. But the teacher must be sufficiently ahead of the students to be able to teach with confidence and understanding, and sufficiently keen on what is being taught to be able to put it over in an interesting and effective manner. To do this the teacher must be well trained in teaching methods applicable to adults and be aware of the needs and feelings of the students and of the society to which they belong. These are the vital attributes.

Essential attributes of the administrator

The Administrator needs to have a thorough understanding of the aims and principles of adult education and of educational administration, planning and financing. To this should be added an understanding of the fundamentals of sociology and a knowledge of teaching methods appropriate for adults. In richer countries, guidance and counselling services are being introduced to enable adults to know what facilities are available for their continuing education. For some time to come this is a service which third world countries will not be able to afford. It is, therefore, essential that those responsible for the administration of adult education should be able to supply information to would-be-consumers. This is especially the case for those working at village and area levels since they are the people in direct contact with the public.

For both administrators and teachers

It has been urged repeatedly that the prime task of adult education is to help people to change. Wrongly handled men and women will not become agents of change; an insensitive approach can cause them to close rather than open their minds to new possibilities. In all training for adult education, therefore, the key factor is to help administrators and teachers to be sensitive to the feelings of those they are seeking to serve. Right relationships are all important; adults are people with minds of their own, and it is no use trying to treat them either as children or as animated robots.

Types of Training

Training courses of some variety will be required for the differing categories of personnel engaged in adult education. These are summarized in Table 7 and are concerned mainly with pedagogical and administrative matters. In addition those who have teaching responsibilities will require training in their own disciplines, since it is essential that they are fully competent in their subjects. As the activities will be very diverse the services of specialists competent to teach at various levels will be required. National vocational training centres, for example, may need high-level engineers; area mobile teams may be better served by skilled motor mechanics. In most cases teaching will be done by people having the necessary skills working on a part-time basis. When it comes to the large number of teachers at the basic level of general education the same rule applies. The teacher of illiterates must be able to read, write and do simple computations and to have the appropriate pedagogical skills which enables the teaching to be effective.

TABLE 7. *Training courses in adult education*

Institution	Types of courses	Staff	Students
University	(a) Long-term (1/2 years) professional course (b) Short seminars on aspects of adult education, and/or for specific target groups	(i) Department of Adult Education (University) (ii) Other university staff (iii) Other people involved in adult education	(a) Those wishing to make adult education their career (b) Policy-makers, government officials, specialists
National Training Centre	(a) Medium-term ($\pm$ 6 months) professional course (b) Short workshops on aspects of adult education (c) Short workshops for specific target groups	(i) Staff of the Centre (ii) AE specialists in the Ministry (iii) Staff of other ministries (iv) Staff of radio, T.V., film unit	(a) Full-time workers for whom longer, university course is not appropriate (b) Specialists, advisers, full-time teachers (c) Script writers, film makers
Provincial Centre	Short training courses, work-shops, seminars	(i) Provincial, area staff (ii) University staff (iii) Others involved in adult education	Part-time teachers, Local Government officials Leaders Officials in voluntary organizations, co-ops, trade unions, etc.
Area	Very short training courses	Area staff and others	Part-time teachers
Teacher Training Colleges	Part of normal teacher-training	Provincial, area staff	Teachers in training

Courses at the University

In many countries the training of adult educationists was pioneered by the national university. This was because governments had failed to recognize the need to make provision of this kind, parallel to the teacher-training institutions for those destined to teach the young. It is to the credit of universities that they accepted this task; in many instances this has led them to continue with work which would now be better done by other institutions, indeed it could be argued that the continuance of universities pre-empting this field has undoubtedly retarded the establishment of training centres specifically for adult educationists.

Universities have an important role to play in training, and should be given the resources to fulfil it. First and foremost the staff of the University Department of Adult Education, augmented by colleagues working in other disciplines such as sociology and psychology, are ideally placed to offer long-term professional courses of study extending over at least 1 and if possible 2 years. Courses such as these have been established in many of the developing countries, though the distribution is patchy with a concentration on the English-speaking countries of Africa.[5] The syllabuses tend to vary between universities reflecting particular interests, though there is a discernible core to all the courses embracing study of the principles of adult education, adult psychology, sociology, teaching methods, and educational planning and administration. Examples of three such courses are given in Table 8.

University courses of the kind described are for those who intend making adult education their career. Entry to them should be either in accordance with the normal admission requirements of the institution or under special mature age entry regulations in which paper qualifications are lowered or waived altogether if balanced by a period of satisfactory working experience in adult education.

Whilst including the underlying theoretical background, it is essential that all training courses for full-time staff should emphasize the importance of studying the subject in the context of the community in which the trainee is to work. To this end there is value in structuring the course so that short periods of intensive study in the university are followed by times of supervised practical work in the field.

---

[5]A list of universities offering such courses is given in *Universities and Adult Education, Research and Training: A Survey* by E. K. Townsend Coles, ICUAE, Aug. 1970.

TABLE 10. *Examples of adult education one-year diploma courses at three universities*

University	General	History	Sociology	Psychology	Teaching methods	Programme	Administration	Other
Dar-es-Salaam (1)	Scope, role and purpose of AE Contemporary AE	AE in Tanzania		Adult learning	Methods of teaching adults Teaching practice	Literacy	Planning and administration of AE	Radio education Correspondence education Political education Rural development Workers' education Applied research methods Concept of development
Nairobi (2)	AE Foundations	Comparative AE		Adult learning	Communication; special methods in teaching adults. Audio-visual aids		Planning and administration	
Rajasthan (3)	Principles of AE	Historical perspectives	Sociological background of AE	Adult psychology and adult learning	Methods of AE	Planning organization and administration of AE programmes		

In some cases the classification of subjects has been somewhat arbitrary since several disciplines are involved.
(1) From St.NO.TD.2711 of 12.5.75.
(2) From University of Nairobi, Diploma course in adult education, 3.10.75.
(3) From *Universities and Adult Education Research and Training: A Survey*, E. K. Townsend Coles, International Congress of University Adult Education, August 1970, p. 42(c).

During these times instruction would be mainly by correspondence, with the assignments related directly to the local community.

There is much to be said for those intending to work wholly in adult education having a 6 to 9 months' probationary period of practical administrative and teaching duties before commencing training. This is particularly important where full-time courses are so concentrated that there is little time available for practical work. During this probationary period the trainees should be under the personal supervision of an experienced educationist.

It is assumed that sponsors of students of these long-term training courses will provide grants to cover fees and maintenance costs. For government-sponsored students, they should be on the same footing as those entering teacher-training colleges. Industrial undertakings, trade unions, co-operatives, political parties, churches and voluntary organizations should be encouraged to set aside funds to pay for students in training as adult educationists.

In addition to long-term courses leading to qualifications, University Departments of Adult Education ought also to be arranging short seminars and workshops on a variety of subjects requiring participation from staff of various faculties. These short courses would be for different groups concerned with adult education, provoking thought on current issues and providing a means of disseminating the results of research. Two groups of potential participants at such seminars deserve to be singled out for special mention. These are the political leaders of a country and secondly senior functionaires in the civil service. There is an urgent need for both to have an understanding of adult education and the part which it plays in national development. The university provides a good forum in which such discussions could take place.

National Resource and Training Centre

The training wing of the Centre (described in Chapter 5) will be responsible for providing two kinds of courses. First there should be a relatively long and intensive course of about 6 months duration. This will be for those who intend working full-time in adult education but for whom the 1- or 2- year course in the university would not be suitable because the person cannot be spared for such lengthy training, or has formerly completed a teacher training course and only requires reorientation to the special needs of adults, or for whom a university course would be at too high an academic level. There will thus be a considerable demand for such a course which should focus on practical issues concerned with administration and programming of adult education and the teaching of adults.

The second category of courses at the Centre would be short workshops and seminars of great variety, many of them as part of a carefully designed programme of inservice retraining and refresher courses for those in adult education and also for teachers and administrators in the formal system. Some seminars would be for specialists in branches of adult education; others would be for part-time teachers dealing with problems associated with the teaching of their specific subjects, a provision often neglected especially for teachers of vocational skills; others would be occasions for writers and illustrators concerned with publications for adults, and especially of books for new literates; and others for writers of correspondence courses and compilers of scripts for television and radio programmes. The list of suitable areas for such seminars is limitless. It is important that those responsible for the Centre should be discerning what are the priority areas to be tackled.

The number of training centres, National and/or Provincial, which a country needs will obviously vary according to the size of the population being served and the funds available. Where no such Centre exists in a country it would be wise to start with one on an experimental basis.

There is much to be said for those working in adult education but not under the jurisdiction of the Ministry of Education to receive their pedagogical training at such a Centre. Community development, agricultural extension and public health officials are as much adult educationists as their colleagues in the Ministry of Education. Where a Centre is able to do this it is serving an important public service by promoting co-operation between the agencies; it also becomes a much more financially attractive proposition to Treasury officials.

Provincial Training

Training at the provincial level may or may not take place in buildings set aside solely for the purpose; this will depend on the approach a country adopts towards adult education and the resources available. Borrowed premises can serve quite adequately as centres for the training of part-time teachers and leaders.

To start from the grass-roots, part-time village and community leaders will need training to prepare them for their role as local catalysts. Leaders are not specialists; their task is primarily to act as middlemen between those in need and those who can provide. They should have some instruction in teaching methods, with special emphasis on whatever is most likely to be needed in their locality and also in simple administrative practices. Information on adult education facilities should be included so that they can give guidance to those seeking details of what is available. Much of the collecting of elementary data for statistical purposes will be done by leaders and they will need advice on how and what to do. As most leaders are likely to be schoolteachers, such courses will probably have to be arranged during school holidays, or over a series of week-ends. It would be a sensible act of generosity for leaders to receive some financial remuneration for undergoing training.

Part-time teachers, and particularly for those working with illiterates, will also need training. Since many who volunteer for the work are not likely to be highly educated themselves, they will not be able to take in too much advice all at one time. For instance, in the initial training course for teachers of illiterates they should learn the general methods to be employed and be given practice in several of the actual lessons. But it would be essential for the teachers to be called together regularly by leaders, with the help of the AAEO, for further guidance so that problems which have arisen could be discussed. No training should ever be regarded as a once-for-all experience; at all levels continued in-service and refresher courses, sometimes of only a few hours' duration, will be needed.

Quite a different training function might also be provided at the provincial level. This is training in study methods for students who are working alone on formal correspondence courses. Such occasions are especially valuable for those who are commencing disciplined work after an interval away from school. The drop-out rate of correspondence students might be appreciably lowered if a little time is devoted to advising students on how best to set about their work.

Teacher-training Colleges

Teachers are usually amongst the animateurs in the community. Whether or not a teacher intends helping with adult education, it is important that all in the profession are aware of the contribution which this branch of education is making. Furthermore, it is essential to strengthen the links between the formal and non-formal systems. Some mention should therefore be made of adult education during normal teacher-training courses, as also some understanding of the formal system should figure in training courses for adult educationists.

Research

Staff have to be trained for their work in adult education. Such training, however, must be oriented towards the real needs of society and the teaching methods and aids proposed must be effective. If adult educationists are to do their work properly, their training must be based on factual information supported by objective evaluation of what is being undertaken.

In the minds of many the word research implies some rarefied and abstruse operation, fit only for staff of universities. Undoubtedly much of the research, especially of an experimental kind, will have to be undertaken in universities. Many research projects are interdisciplinary and the researcher in a university will have the benefit of consulting colleagues studying subjects other than his own.

But it is equally certain that much research should be carried out by educationists not in a university. Lowe has suggested that "one must see that everybody involved at any level in adult education is research-minded".[6] Not that everyone need be a specialist. Much of the research is of a descriptive kind and involves the systematic collection of data, together with observation of activities and the recording of what is seen to have happened.

Statistics

Adult education is the most poorly recorded of all branches of edu-

---

[6]*Programmed Learning and Research in Adult Education*, Conference Proceedings, 1966. *Adult Education Association of East and Central Africa*, Nairobi, p. 77 (J. Lowe, The main areas of research).

cation. It is not uncommon for there to be an almost total absence of statistics on adult classes and other activities, and often those which are available are highly suspect, having been compiled less from fact and more from fancy. It is essential that every country should adopt procedures for the collection of data on adult education, not only from the statutory providers but from other sources as well. This is not an easy task; the field is complicated and confused. Unesco has recently published guidelines on the collection of statistics for adult education[7] and it is hoped that these will stimulate countries to be more active over the collection of data.

The statistics collected should be collated and published, work which is likely to be a responsibility of the national Department of Adult Education in the Ministry. They can then be made available to universities and regional and international organizations for analysis and for use in comparative studies.

Evaluation

One aspect of research which has received a great deal of public attention in recent years is that of evaluation. There has been a growing realization that much formal education has developed without there ever being any objective examination of the results achieved; the same can also be said of non-formal and adult education. In recent years the need for on-going evaluation has been emphasized. In part this has come about because of the failure of so much literacy teaching, involving large sums of money, resulting in disappointing results.

At all levels there should be evaluation. A teacher or leader should be constantly evaluating the impact of his work; participants should be encouraged to be articulate on the failures and successes of a particular enterprise. Administrators should be equally observant and objective, and from time to time, the university should be called in to give assistance. Realistic evaluation of activities should lead to the planning of more appropriate and valuable programmes in the future.

At the same time evaluation must not get out of hand; it should not become the panacea of adult education, and evaluation studies should be conducted in a manner likely to produce useful and practical

---

[7]*Manual for the Collection of Adult Education Statistics* (CSR/E/15), Unesco, Paris, 1975.

results, whether of a negative or a positive kind, and with sufficient speed so that the findings can be used to correct errors.

Directories and Year Books

A Directory or Year Book, listing the kind of information which people working in adult education will require—and available also to the general public—is a very valuable resource document and one which should be produced by the Department in the Ministry. The publication should include the addresses of organizations concerned with adult education as well as sources of supply of teaching aids, films, slides, etc. It is surprising how ignorant people are of such information.

Journals

The value of comparative studies in adult education is now recognized, even if there is danger that events recorded in one country may be introduced into another without due thought of the adaptations needed. Unfortunately, it is the reverse which is often the case; of educationists being unaware of the results obtained from the work of colleagues in other countries. Valuable material may thus be wasted, and countries indulge in experimentation blindfold without heeding the experiences of others. To some extent this problem is being overcome by the publication of several international journals, and by the adult education abstracting service offered by Unesco.[8]

Every country should have its own national publication in adult education. This is not a frill but rather an essential vehicle for the exchange of ideas and for encouraging a sense of identity and *esprit de corps* amongst those working in adult education. A publication of this kind need not be costly. A duplicated news-letter is adequate though a printed document is more likely to be read.

It has already been suggested that there should be a national resource centre in every country. Such a centre would include a library of books, journals, articles and off-prints filed in such a way as to facilitate speedy retrieval.

---

[8]Co-operative Educational Abstracting Service (CEAS), Adult Education Series, International Bureau of Education, Palais Wilson, Geneva, Switzerland.

The Directorate of Adult Education of the Government of India has initiated a good method of keeping staff up to date with news and information. People working in the field are provided with inexpensive file cases, which are divided into several different sections, each one for some specific topic or type of information, such as publications, teaching methods, etc.

The Directorate mails loose papers to staff containing information which can then be filed and kept in the appropriate section of the folder. This system allows for a constant flow of material to be going out to workers and it makes up-dating of information a comparatively inexpensive procedure.

CHAPTER 7

Delivering the Goods

The preceding five chapters have consisted of a catalogue of ideas concerning adult education; the time has now come to draw these together so that the final vision is one of a coherent whole.

An Analogy with Commerce

In commercial terms, what has been done is to describe some marketable goods and how to deliver them to the potential customers. This analogy must not be taken too far; there are times when things have to be done which no businessman would think of doing; there is a difference between crude commerce and education. Nevertheless, it is time that educationists took heed how their commercial counterparts go about their tasks, for many valuable lessons can be learned. Nobody running a firm—and this must surely be true for both socialist and capitalist societies—would prepare something for the market without first doing detailed research to find out if the product is likely to be wanted. That is to say, the customer is at the centre of their attention. Care, too, must be taken to present the object in a form most likely to be acceptable, in a place where it is needed and at a time when the potential customers are most likely to be interested in making a purchase. This means that there has to be adequate publicity under-guided by an efficient delivery system; and there has to be some way of finding out, as quickly as possible, whether the customers are satisfied.

Now consider education. Is similar care taken over the preparation and marketing of what is on offer? Sadly the answer is almost invariably no, and the reason for this is not hard to find. Educationists have had it all their own way; at least until some students made their voices heard and demanded action. It has not mattered if the product is out of date, irrelevant and meaningless, nor if the methods adopted were ineffective and tedious, the place of business dull and forbidding, and the end product ill-equipped for what it is intended to do. None of these considerations were important because come what may children would continue to go to school; partly because the law said they must; partly because parents believed that the medicine would work a miracle; and partly because the children themselves were docile and willing.

This state of affairs, amounting to a colossal waste of time, energy and money might be pardonable in affluent societies; it is wholly unpardonable in the poor countries where all resources have to be carefully husbanded. And fortunately the practice is changing; changing in child education as also in adult education, though in the latter because the act is voluntarily made by the participants, some small care has always had to be taken with the right way of delivering the goods. At last it is being recognized that the customer, the learner, is the subject and not the object of education.

The marketing of adult education, set aside its commercial counterpart, would thus be broadly as shown in Table 11.

Another way of representing the translation of ideas into programmes is given in Diagram 14. In this somewhat simplified case the ideas stemming both from citizens and from the government are fed into the various providing agencies, mostly governmental, who produce programme material. This material is assembled in the form of teaching sets, publications, newspapers, films and programmes on radio and television. An intermediary administrative level eases problems of distribution and allows for a focus for information and feedback.

This is not, of course, the whole picture. For the educational flow to take place there has to be a well-developed delivery system. Unfortunately, because of pressing demands, there is a tendency to wish to start operations before a system has been designed, or in commercial terms, to produce and market some goods quickly without making sure that all the other processes between producer and consumer will function efficiently. In the short run of course, to do so will appear to produce good results. Many literacy campaigns have been originated in this manner. Public enthusiasm for learning to read and write is generated and classes begin before adequate pre-

TABLE 11. *The marketing of adult education*

The commercial pattern	The educational counterpart
1. Market research	1. Citizens saying what they want Governments announcing their priorities and aims Ideas incorporating both are fed to
2. Manufacture of a prototype	2. Ministry of Education Educational Resource Centres Teacher-training Colleges University Departments of Adult Education Vocational Training Establishments All potential providers who produce some draft proposals
3. Testing of prototype	3. and try them out
4. Main production	4. Finally, after any necessary changes have been made, what- ever materials required are produced at the same time
5. Preparation of salesman Advertising Ensuring that delivery system works	5. Preparing Letting Ensuring teachers people that the know delivery system will work so that
6. Marketing the product	6. The activities can take place, followed by a
7. Consumer reaction	7. Careful evaluation of the results by the providing agencies.
8. Modifications Marketing continues	8. Modifications are made and further programmes produced.

paration has been made for the production of follow-up literature. The immediate result is superficially satisfying and statistically praiseworthy; hundreds of people made literate. It is only when the long-term effects are perceived, and these can only become apparent some

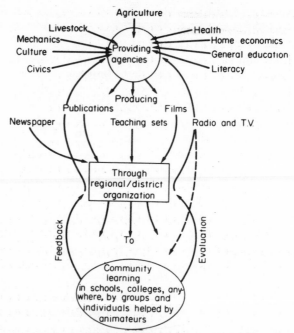

DIAGRAM 14. A diagrammatic representation of adult education
(taken from *Somalia: Non-Formal Education*, by E. K. Townsend
Coles, E. Gunnarsen, A. Shaw and G. Thomas, Unesco, Paris,
1974, p. 17).

years later, it will be realized that much of the effort has resulted in
little lasting improvement. Like the child who has had to leave
primary school too soon, the adult literate, having nothing to encourage retention of the newly gained knowledge, will soon sink back
into illiteracy but with the added hindrance to any future opportunities
to learn of a sense of frustration bred out of the realization that the
initial experience has been largely wasted.

It is thus essential to make sure that there is a sound delivery system
and one which is flexible enough to be able to change with and respond
to the varying circumstances which will be encountered.

The Delivery System

The delivery system in adult education consists of a number of interrelated parts. Like the pieces of a watch it is only when they are all correctly assembled that the mechanism does what is intended of it. It can probably malfunction if a few pieces are missing; the time can be read, for example, even when the minute hand is broken, though with impaired accuracy; but at best the action will only be partially effective.

Unfortunately, far too little thought is given to ensuring that there is an efficient delivery system in adult education. Often parts are well-developed, whilst others are neglected. Sometimes bottlenecks occur because quite small component parts have been overlooked. A common example of this is the lack of adequate transportation for teachers, supervisors and materials.

The delivery system consists of the diverse components which have been described in the preceding chapters. It thus includes a structural framework in which all the providers can both make their own individual contributions and also work co-operatively together for the common good; adequate staffing, together with facilities for training and retraining; the mobilization of people to teach; material resources in sufficient quantity and of the right kind in the right place; the fullest use of all the means of communication; efficient channels of feedback and the application of realistic methods of evaluation; and above all enabling the learners to play their full part in programme planning and implementation.

In 1975 Unesco in association with the African Adult Education Association, sponsored a seminar on structures of adult education[1] in developing countries, with special reference to Africa. The report of this seminar contains seventeen resolutions which taken together form a checklist on what is required to establish an effective system of adult education. The resolutions are reprinted as Appendix C to this book. Whilst they do not claim to be wholly exhaustive in their scope they do refer to the main components which are needed.

Only when such a system is established is it reasonable to expect the public as a whole to take the concept of continuing education seriously, for only then will they have confidence that their educational needs throughout life will be met. When this position is reached there will be

---

[1]*Seminar on Structures of Adult Education in Developing Countries with special reference to Africa. Final Report,* Unesco, Paris, 1975.

some hope that the formal system of education for children and adolescents will be able to break out of the prison into which it has allowed itself to become ensnared. For at last the time will have come when schooling can cease to be an intensive and increasingly futile cramming process and instead be transformed into a preparation for life in the modern world.

Then formal and non-formal (adult) education will be able, amicably, to join forces and together to be "the servicing agent of change and development".[2] The one will not be taking over the unfinished business of the other, but both will have but a single aim. Education will be reunited with life and with the realities of living, and people—all people, men, women and children—will be helped to "live satisfying lives in their environment, make the most effective use of their talents and skills" . . . and to be inspired "to serve their communities, their societies and their countries".[2]

[2]Miss F. H. Guilliam, C.B.E., Presidential Address, Education Section of the British Association, 1967.

Declaration of the Montreal World Conference on Adult Education[1]

The destruction of mankind and the conquest of space have both become technological possibilities to our present generation. These are the most dramatic forms of technological development, but they are not the only ones. New industrial methods, new means of communication are affecting all parts of the world, and industrialisation and urbanisation are overtaking areas that twenty years ago were rural and agricultural. Nor are the changes which are going to fashion the pattern of our lives during the remainder of this century only in technology. In great areas of the world the population is increasing fast, new national states are emerging, and much of the world has become divided, within the last few years, into rival camps. Every generation has its own problems; in sober fact no previous generation has been faced with the extent and rapidity of change which faces and challenges us.

Our first problem is to survive. It is not a question of the survival of the fittest; either we survive together, or we perish together. Survival requires that the countries of the world must learn to live together in peace. "Learn" is the operative word. Mutual respect, understanding, sympathy are qualities that are destroyed by ignorance and fostered by knowledge. In the field of international understanding, adult education in today's divided world takes on a new importance. Provided that man learns to survive, he has in front of him opportunities for social development and personal well-being such as have never been open to him before.

---

[1]*Educational Studies and Documents,* No. 46. Second World Conference on Adult Education. Declaration of the Montreal World Conference on Adult Education. Unesco, 1963, p. 11. '

The rapidly developing countries in Asia, Africa and Latin America have their own special problems. For them, adult education, including education for literacy, is an immediate need, a need so overpowering that here and now we must help adult men and women to acquire the knowledge and the skills that they need for the new patterns of community living into which they are moving. These developing countries have few immediately available resources, and great demands on them.

The countries which are better off have an opportunity of helping those which are poorer; they have the opportunity of performing such an act of wisdom, justice and generosity as could seize the imagination of the whole world. With their help illiteracy could be eradicated within a few years, if, preferably through the United Nations and its agencies, a resolute, comprehensive and soundly planned campaign were undertaken. We believe profoundly that this is an opportunity which ought to be seized.

But it is not only in the developing countries that adult education is needed. In the developed countries the need for vocational and technical training is increasingly accepted, but that is not enough. Healthy societies are composed of men and women, not of animated robots, and there is a danger, particularly in the developed countries, that the education of adults may get out of balance by emphasizing too much vocational needs and technical skills. Man is a many-sided being, with many needs. They must not be met piecemeal and in adult education programmes they must all be reflected. Those powers of mind and those qualities of spirit which have given to mankind an abiding heritage of values and judgement must continue everywhere to find, in our changing patterns of day-to-day living, full scope for maturing and flowering in an enriched culture. This and nothing less is the goal of adult education.

We believe that adult education has become of such importance for man's survival and happiness that a new attitude towards it is needed. Nothing less will suffice than that people everywhere should come to accept adult education as a normal, and that governments should treat it as a necessary, part of the educational provision of every country.

Development of Adult Education[1]

Being the draft of a proposed international instrument on the development of adult education to be submitted to the General Conference of Unesco in October/November, 1976.

[1]This document was approved by an inter-governmental meeting of experts in June 1976, and will be submitted to the 19th session of the General Conference of UNESCO for ratification in October/November 1976. Document 19C/24. Copyright. Unesco, 1976. Reprinted by permission of Unesco.

DRAFT RECOMMENDATION ON THE
DEVELOPMENT OF ADULT EDUCATION

The General Conference of the United Nations Educational, Scientific and Cultural Organization, meeting in . . . . from . . . . to . . . . 1976, at its nineteenth session,

Recalling the principles set forth in Articles 26 and 27 of the Universal Declaration of Human Rights, guaranteeing and specifying the right of everyone to education and to participate freely in cultural, artistic and scientific life and the principles set forth in Articles 13 and 15 of the International Covenant on Economic, Social and Cultural Rights,

Considering that education is inseparable from democracy, the abolition of privilege and the promotion within society as a whole of the ideas of autonomy, responsibility and dialogue,

Considering that the access of adults to education, in the context of life-long education, is a fundamental aspect of the right to education and facilitates the exercise of the right to participate in political, cultural, artistic and scientific life,

Considering that for the full development of the human personality, particularly in view of the rapid pace of scientific, technical, economic and social change, education must be considered on a global basis and as a life-long process,

Considering that the development of adult education, in the context of life-long education, is necessary as a means of achieving a more rational and more equitable distribution of educational resources between young people and adults, and between different social groups, and of ensuring better understanding and more effective collaboration between the generations and greater political, social and economic equality between social groups and between the sexes,

Convinced that adult education as an integral part of life-long education can contribute decisively to economic and cultural development, social progress and world peace as well as to the development of educational systems,

Considering that the experience acquired in adult education must constantly contribute to the renewal of educational methods, as well as to the reform of educational systems as a whole,

Considering the universal concern for literacy as being a crucial factor in political and economic development, in technological progress, and in social and cultural change, so that its promotion should therefore form an integral part of any plan for adult education,

Reaffirming that the attainment of this objective entails creating situations in which the adults are able to choose, from among a variety of forms of educational activity the objectives and content of which have been defined with their collaboration, those forms which meet their needs most closely and are most directly related to their interests,

Bearing in mind the diversity of modes of training and education throughout the world and the special problems peculiar to the countries whose education systems are as yet underdeveloped or insufficiently adapted to national needs,

In order to give effect to the conclusions, declarations and recommendations formulated by the second and third international conferences on adult education (Montreal, 1960; Tokyo, 1972), and as far as the relevant paragraphs are concerned, by the World Conference of the International Women's Year (Mexico, 1975),

Desirous of making a further contribution to putting into effect the principles set forth in the recommendations addressed by the International Conference on Public Education to the Ministries of Education concerning the access of women to education (Recommendation No. 34, 1952), facilities for education in rural areas (Recommendation No. 47, 1958), and literacy and adult education (Recommendation No. 58, 1965), in the Declaration adopted at the International Symposium for Literacy in Persepolis (1975), and in the Recommendation concerning Education for International Understanding, Co-operation and Peace and Education relating to Human Rights and Fundamental Freedoms adopted by the General Conference at its eighteenth session (1974),

Taking note of the provisions of the Revised Recommendation concerning Technical and Vocational Education adopted by the General Conference at its eighteenth session (1974) and of resolution 3.426 adopted at the same session with a view to the adoption of an international instrument concerning action designed to ensure that the people at large have free democratic access to culture and an opportunity to take an active part in the cultural life of society,

Noting further that the International Labour Conference has adopted a number of instruments concerned with various aspects of adult education, and in particular the recommendation on vocational guidance (1949), the recommendation on vocational training in agriculture (1956), as well as the conventions and recommendations concerning paid educational leave (1974), and of human resources development (1975),

Having decided, at its eighteenth session, that adult education would be the subject of a recommendation to Member States,

Adopts the present recommendation this . . . . .day of . . . . 1976.

The General Conference recommends that Member States apply the following provisions by taking whatever legislative or other steps may be required, and in conformity with the constitutional practice of each State, to give effect to the principles set forth in this Recommendation.

The General Conference recommends that Member States bring this Recommendation to the attention of the authorities, departments or bodies responsible for adult education and also of the various organizations carrying out educational work for the benefit of adults, and of trade union organizations, associations, enterprises, and other interested parties.

The General Conference recommends that Member States report to it, at such dates and in such form as shall be determined by it, on the action taken by them in pursuance of this Recommendation.

I.   DEFINITION

1.   In this Recommendation:

the term "adult education" denotes the entire body of organized educational processes, whatever the content, level and method, whether formal or otherwise, whether they prolong or replace initial education in schools, colleges and universities as well as in apprenticeship, whereby persons regarded as adult by the society to which they belong develop their abilities, enrich their knowledge, improve their technical or professional qualifications and bring about changes in their attitudes or behaviour in the twofold perspective of full personal development and participation in balanced and independent social, economic and cultural development;

adult education, however, must not be considered as an entity in itself; it is a sub-division, and an integral part of, a global scheme for life-long education and learning;

the term "life-long education and learning", for its part, denotes an overall scheme aimed both at restructuring the existing education system and at developing the entire educational potential outside the education system;

in such a scheme men and women are the agents of their own education, through continual interaction between their thoughts and actions;

education and learning, far from being limited to the period of attendance at school, should extend throughout life, include all skills and branches of knowledge, use all possible means, and give the opportunity to all people for full development of the personality;

the educational and learning processes in which children, young people and adults of all ages are involved in the course of their lives, in whatever form, should be considered as a whole.

II.   OBJECTIVES AND STRATEGY

2.   Generally speaking, the aims of adult education should be to contribute to:

(a) promoting work for peace, international understanding and co-operation;

(b) developing a critical understanding of major contemporary problems and social changes and the ability to play an active part in the progress of society with a view to achieving social justice;

(c) promoting increased awareness of the relationship between people and their physical and cultural environment, and fostering the desire to improve the environment and to respect and protect nature, the common heritage and public property;

(d) creating an understanding of and respect for the diversity of customs and cultures, on both the national and the international planes;

(e) promoting increased awareness of, and giving effect to various forms of communication and solidarity at the family, local, national, regional and international levels;

(f) developing the aptitude for acquiring, either individually, in groups, or in the context of organized study in educational establishments specially set up for this purpose, new knowledge, qualifications, attitudes or forms of behaviour conducive to the full maturity of the personality;

(g) ensuring the individuals' conscious and effective incorporation into working life by providing men and women with an advanced technical and vocational education and developing the ability to create, either individually or in groups, new material goods and new spiritual or aesthetic values;

(h) developing the ability to grasp adequately the problems involved in the upbringing of children;

(i) developing the aptitude for making creative use of leisure and for acquiring any necessary or desired knowledge;

(j) developing the necessary discernment in using mass communication media, in particular radio, television, cinema and the press, and interpreting the various messages addressed to modern men and women by society;

(k) developing the aptitude for learning to learn.

3. Adult education should be based on the following principles:

(a) it should be based on the needs of the participants and make use of their different experiences in the development of adult education; the most educationally underprivileged groups should be given the highest priority within a perspective of collective advancement;

(b) it should rely on the ability and determination of all human beings to make progress throughout their lives both at the level of their personal development and in relation to their social activity;

(c) it should awaken an interest in reading and develop cultural aspirations;

(d) it should stimulate and sustain the interest of adult learners, appeal to their experience, strengthen their self-reliance, and enlist their active participation at all stages of the educational process in which they are involved;

(e) it should be adapted to the actual conditions of everyday life and work and take into account the personal character- istics of adult learners, their age, family, social, occupational or residential background and the way in which these inter- relate;

(f) it should seek the participation of individual adults, groups and communities in decision-making at all levels of the learn- ing process; including determination of needs, curriculum development, programme implementation and evaluation and should plan educational activities with a view to the transformation of the working environment and of the life of adults;

(g) it should be organized and operated flexibly by taking into account social, cultural, economic and institutional factors of each country and society to which adult learners belong;

(h) it should contribute to the economic and social development of the entire community;

(i) it should recognize as an integral part of the educational pro- cess the forms of collective organization established by adults with a view to solving their day-to-day problems;

(j) it should recognize that every adult, by virtue of his or her experience of life, is the vehicle of a culture which enables him or her to play the rôle of both learner and teacher in the educational process in which he or she participates.

4.   Each Member State should:

(a) recognize adult education as a necessary and specific component of its education system and as a permanent element in its social, cultural and economic development policy; it should, consequently, promote the creation of structures, the preparation and implementation of programmes and the application of educational methods which meet the needs and aspirations of all categories of adults, without restriction on grounds of sex, race, geographical origin, age, social status, opinion, belief or prior educational standard;

(b) in eliminating the isolation of women from adult education, should work towards ensuring equality of access and full participation in the entire range of adult education activities, including those which provide training for qualifications leading to activities or responsibilities which have hitherto been reserved for men;

(c) take measures with a view to promoting participation in adult education and community development programmes by members of the most underprivileged groups, whether rural or urban, settled or nomadic, and in particular illiterates, young people who have been unable to acquire an adequate standard of general education or a qualification, migrant workers and refugees, unemployed workers, members of ethnic minorities, persons suffering from a physical or mental handicap, persons experiencing difficulties of social adjustment and those serving prison sentences. In this context Member States should associate themselves in the search for educational strategies designed to foster more equitable relations among social groups;

(d) recognize that although, in a given situation or for a specific period, adult education may play a compensatory rôle, it is not intended as a substitute for adequate youth education which is a prerequisite for the full success of adult education.

5. The place of adult education in each education system should be defined with a view to achieving:

(a) a rectification of the main inequalities in access to initial education and training, in particular inequalities based on age, sex, social position or social or geographical origin;

(b) the assurance of a scientific basis for life-long education and learning as well as greater flexibility in the way in which people divide their lives beteen education and work, and, in particular, providing for the alternation of periods of education and work throughout the life-span, and facilitating the integration of continuing education into the activity of work itself;

(c) recognition, and increased exploitation, of the actual or potential educational value of the adult's various experiences;

(d) easy transfer from one type or level of education to another;

(e) greater interaction between the education system and its social, cultural and economic setting;

(f) greater efficiency from the point of view of the contribution of educational expenditure to social, cultural and economic development.

6. Consideration should be given to the need for an adult education component, including literacy, in the framing and execution of any development programme.

7. The objectives and goals of adult education policy should be incorporated in national development plans; they should be defined in relation to the overall objectives of education policy and of social, cultural and economic development policies.

Adult education and other forms of education, particularly

school and higher education and initial vocational training, should be conceived and organized as equally essential components in a co-ordinated but differentiated education system according to the tenets of life-long education and learning.

8. Measures should be taken to encourage the public authorities, institutions or bodies engaged in education, voluntary associations, workers' and employers' organizations, and those directly participating in adult education, to collaborate in the task of defining further and giving effect to these objectives.

III. CONTENT OF ADULT EDUCATION

9. Adult education activities, viewed as forming part of life-long education and learning, have no theoretical boundaries and should meet the particular situations created by the specific needs of development, of participation in community life and of individual self-fulfilment; they cover all aspects of life and all fields of knowledge and are addressed to all people whatever their level of achievement. In defining the content of adult education activities priority should be given to the specific needs of the educationally most underprivileged groups.

10. Civic, political, trade union and co-operative education activities should be aimed particularly towards developing independent and critical judgement and implanting or enhancing the abilities required by each individual in order to cope with changes affecting living and working conditions, by effective participation in the management of social affairs at every level of the decision-making process.

11. While not excluding approaches intended to achieve a short-term solution in a particular situation, technical and vocational education activities should as a general rule emphasize the acquisition of qualifications which are sufficiently broad to allow of subsequent changes of occupation and a critical understanding of the problems of working life. It is necessary to integrate

general and civic education with technical and vocational education.

12. Activities designed to promote cultural development and artistic creation should encourage appreciation of existing cultural and artistic values and works and, at the same time, should aim to promote the creation of new values and new works, by releasing the expressive capabilities inherent in each individual or group.

13. Participation in adult education should not be restricted on grounds of sex, race, geographical origin, culture, age, social status, experience, belief and prior educational standard.

13.1 With regard to women, adult education activities should be integrated as far as possible with the whole contemporary social movement directed towards achieving self-determination for women and enabling them to contribute to the life of society as a collective force, and should thus focus specifically on certain aspects, in particular:

(a) the establishment in each society of conditions between men and women on an "equal-but-different" basis;

(b) the emancipation of women from the masculine models imposed on them by society in every field in which they carry responsibility;

(c) civic, occupational, psychological, cultural and economic autonomy for women as a necessary condition for their existence as complete individuals;

(d) knowledge about the status of women, and about women's movements, in various societies, with a view to increased solidarity across frontiers.

13.2 With regard to settled or nomadic rural populations, adult education activities should be designed in particular to:

(a) enable them to use technical procedures and methods of individual or joint organization likely to improve their standard of living without obliging them to forgo their own values;

(b) put an end to the isolation of individuals or groups;

(c) prepare individuals or groups of individuals who are obliged, despite the efforts made to prevent excessive depopulation of rural areas, to leave agriculture, either to engage in a new occupational activity while remaining in a rural environment, or to leave this environment for a new way of life.

13.3 With regard to such persons or groups as have remained illiterate or are experiencing difficulty in adjusting to society because of the slenderness of their resources, their limited education or their restricted participation in community life, adult education activities should be designed not only to enable them to acquire basic knowledge (reading, writing, arithmetic, basic understanding of natural and social phenomena), but also to make it easier for them to engage in productive work, to promote their self-awareness and their grasp of the problems of hygiene, health, household management and the upbringing of children, and to enhance their autonomy and increase their participation in community life.

13.4 With regard to young people who have been unable to acquire an adequate standard of general education or a qualification, adult education activities should, in particular, enable them to acquire additional general education with a view to developing their ability to understand the problems of society and shoulder social responsibilities, and to gaining access to the vocational training and general education which are necessary for the exercise of an occupational activity.

13.5 If people wish to acquire educational or vocational qualifications which are formally attested by certificates of education or of vocational aptitude and which, for social or economic reasons, they have not been able to obtain earlier, adult education should enable them to obtain the training required for the award of such certificates.

13.6 With regard to the physically or mentally handicapped, adult education activities should be designed, in particular, to restore or offset the physical or mental capacities which have been impaired or lost as a result of their handicap, and to enable them to acquire the knowledge and skills and, where necessary, the professional qualifications required for their social life and for the exercise of an occupational activity compatible with their handicap.

13.7 With regard to migrant workers, refugees, and ethnic minorities, adult education activities should in particular:

(a) enable them to acquire the linguistic and general knowledge as well as the technical or professional qualifications necessary for their temporary or permanent assimilation in the society of the host country and, where appropriate, their reassimilation in the society of their country of origin;

(b) keep them in touch with culture, current developments and social changes in their country of origin.

13.8 With regard to unemployed persons, including the educated unemployed, adult education activities should be designed, in particular, to adapt or modify their technical or professional qualification with a view to enabling them to find or return to employment and to promote a critical understanding of their socio-economic situation.

13.9 With regard to ethnic minorities, adult education activities should enable them to express themselves freely, educate themselves and their children in their mother tongues, develop their own cultures and learn languages other than their mother tongues.

13.10 With regard to the aged, adult education activities should be designed, in particular:

(a) to give all a better understanding of contemporary problems and of the younger generation;

(b) to help acquire leisure skills, promote health, and find increased meaning in life;

(c) to provide a grounding in the problems facing retired people and in ways of dealing with such problems, for the benefit of those who are on the point of leaving working life;

(d) to enable those who have left working life to retain their physical and intellectual faculties and to continue to participate in community life and also to give them access to fields of knowledge or types of activity which have not been open to them during their working life.

IV. METHODS, MEANS, RESEARCH AND EVALUATION

14. Adult education methods should take account of:

(a) incentives and obstacles to participation and learning specially affecting adults;

(b) the experience gained by adults in the exercise of their family, social and occupational responsibilities;

(c) the family, social or occupational obligations borne by adults and the fatigue and impaired alertness which may result from them;

(d) the ability of adults to assume responsibility for their own learning;

(e) the cultural and pedagogical level of the teaching personnel available;

(f) the psychological characteristics of the learning process;

(g) the existence and characteristics of cognitive interests;

(h) use of leisure-time.

15. Adult education activities should normally be planned and executed on the basis of identified needs, problems, wants and resources, as well as defined objectives. Their impact should be evaluated, and reinforced by whatever follow-up activities may be most appropriate to given conditions.

16. Particular emphasis should be placed on adult education activities intended for an entire social or geographical entity, mobilizing all its inherent energies with a view to the advancement of the group and social progress in a community setting.

17. In order to encourage the broadest possible participation, it may be appropriate in some situations to add, to locally based adult education, methods such as:

(a) remote teaching programmes such as correspondence courses and radio or television broadcasts, the intended recipients of such programmes being invited to form groups with a view to listening or working together (such groups should receive appropriate pedagogical support);

(b) programmes launched by mobile units;

(c) self-teaching programmes;

(d) study circles;

(e) use of voluntary work by teachers, students, and other community members.

The various services which public cultural institutions (libraries, museums, record libraries, video-cassette libraries) are able to put at the disposal of adult learners should be developed on a systematic basis, together with new types of institutions specializing in adult education.

18. Participation in an adult education programme should be a voluntary matter. The State and other bodies should strive to

promote the desire of individuals and groups for education in the spirit of life-long education and learning.

19. Relations between the adult learner and the adult educator should be established on a basis of mu^tual respect and co-operation.

20. Participation in an adult education programme should be subject only to the ability to follow the course of training provided and not to any (upper) age limit or any condition concerning the possession of a diploma or qualification; any aptitude tests on the basis of which a selection might be made if necessary should be adapted to the various categories of candidates taking such tests.

21. It should be possible to acquire and accumulate learning, experiences and qualifications through intermittent participation. Rights and qualifications obtained in this way should be equivalent to those granted by the systems of formalized education or of such character as to allow for continued education within this.

22. The methods used in adult education should not appeal to a competitive spirit but should develop in the adult learners a shared sense of purpose and habits of participation, mutual help, collaboration and team work.

23. Adult education programmes for the improvement of technical or professional qualifications should, as far as possible, be organized during working time and, in the case of seasonal work, during the slack season. This should, as a general rule, be applied also to other forms of education, in particular literacy programmes and trade union education.

24. The premises necessary for the development of adult education activities should be provided; depending on the case, these may be premises used exclusively for adult education, with or without residential accommodation, or multi-purpose or integrated facilities or premises generally used or capable of being used for

other purposes—in particular, clubs, workshops, school, university and scientific establishments, social, cultural or sociocultural centres or open air sites.

25. Member States should actively encourage research in all aspects of adult education and its objectives. Research programmes should have a practical basis. They should be carried out by universities, adult education bodies and research bodies, adopting an interdisciplinary approach. Measures should be taken with a view to disseminating the experience and the results of the research programme to those concerned.

26. Systematic evaluation of adult education activities is necessary to secure optimum results from the resources put into them. For evaluation to be effective it should be built into the programmes of adult education at all levels and stages.

V. THE STRUCTURES OF ADULT EDUCATION

27. Member States should endeavour to ensure the establishment and development of a network of bodies meeting the needs of adult education; this network should be sufficiently flexible to meet the various personal and social situations and their evolution.

28. Measures should be taken in order to:

(a) identify and anticipate educational needs capable of being satisfied through adult education programmes;

(b) make full use of existing educational facilities and create such facilities as may be lacking to meet all defined objectives;

(c) make the necessary long-term investments for the development of adult education: in particular for the professional education of planners, administrators, those who train educators, organizational and training personnel, the preparation of educational strategies and methods suitable for adults,

the provision of capital facilities, the production and provision of the necessary basic equipment such as visual aids,
apparatus and technical media;

(d) encourage exchanges of experience and compile and dis-
seminate statistical and other information on the strategies,
structures, contents, methods and results, both quantitative
and qualitative, of adult education;

(e) abolish economic and social obstacles to participation in
education, and to systematically bring the nature and form
of adult education programmes to the attention of all potential beneficiaries, but especially to the most disadvantaged,
by using such means as active canvassing by adult education
institutions and voluntary organizations, to inform, counsel
and encourage possible and often hesitant participants in
adult education.

29. In order to achieve these objectives it will be necessary to
mobilize organizations and institutions specifically concerned
with adult education, and the full range, both public and
private of schools, universities, cultural and scientific establishments, libraries and museums, and, in addition, other institutions not primarily concerned with adult education, such as:

(a) mass information bodies: the press, radio and television;

(b) voluntary associations and consortia;

(c) professional, trade union, family and co-operative organizations;

(d) families;

(e) industrial and commercial firms which may contribute to
the training of their employees;

(f) educators, technicians or qualified experts working on an
individual basis;

(g) any persons or groups who are in a position to make a contribution by virtue of their education, training, experience
or professional or social activities and are both willing and

able to apply the principles set forth in the Preamble and the objectives and strategy outlined in the recommendation;

(h) the adult learners themselves.

30. Member States should encourage schools, vocational education establishments, colleges and institutions of higher education to regard adult education programmes as an integral part of their own activities and to participate in action designed to promote the development of such programmes provided by other institutions, in particular by making available their own teaching staff, conducting research and training the necessary personnel.

VI. TRAINING AND STATUS OF PERSONS ENGAGED IN ADULT EDUCATION WORK

31. It should be recognized that adult education calls for special skills, knowledge, understanding and attitudes on the part of those who are involved in providing it, in whatever capacity and for any purpose. It is desirable therefore that they should be recruited with care according to their particular functions and receive initial and in-service training for them according to their needs and those of the work in which they are engaged.

32. Measures should be taken to ensure that the various specialists who have a useful contribution to make to the work of adult education take part in those activities, whatever their nature or purpose.

33. In addition to the employment of full-time professional workers, measures should be taken to enlist the support of anyone capable of making a contribution, regular or occasional, paid or voluntary, to adult education activities of any kind. Voluntary involvement and participation in all aspects of organizing and teaching are of crucial importance, and people with all kinds of skills are able to contribute to them.

34. Training for adult education should, as far as practicable, in-

clude all those aspects of skill, knowledge, understanding and personal attitude which are relevant to the various functions undertaken, taking into account the general background against which adult education takes place. By integrating these aspects with each other, training should itself be a demonstration of sound adult education practice.

35. Conditions of work and remuneration for full-time staff in adult education should be comparable to those of workers in similar posts elsewhere, and those for paid part-time staff should be appropriately regulated, without detriment to their main occupation.

VII. RELATIONS BETWEEN ADULT EDUCATION AND YOUTH EDUCATION

36. The education of young people should progressively be oriented towards life-long education and learning, taking into account the experience gained in regard to adult education, with a view to preparing young people, whatever their social origins, to take part in adult education or to contribute to providing it.

To this end, measures should be taken with a view to:

(a) making access to all levels of education and training more widely available;

(b) removing the barriers between disciplines and also between types and levels of education;

(c) modifying school and training syllabuses with the aim of maintaining and stimulating intellectual curiosity, and also placing greater emphasis, alongside the acquisition of knowledge, on the development of self-teaching patterns of behaviour, a critical outlook, a reflective attitude and creative abilities;

(d) rendering school institutions of higher education and training establishments increasingly open to their economic and social environment and linking education and work more firmly together;

(e) informing young people at school and young people leaving full-time education or initial training of the opportunities offered by adult education;

(f) bringing together, where desirable, adults and adolescents in the same training programme;

(g) associating youth movements with adult education ventures.

37. In cases where a training course organized as part of adult education leads to the acquisition of a qualification in respect of which a diploma or certificate is awarded when the qualification is acquired through study in school or university, such training should be recognized by the award of a diploma or certificate having equal status. Adult education programmes which do not lead to the acquisition of a qualification similar to those in respect of which a diploma or certificate is awarded should, in appropriate cases, be recognized by an award.

38. Adult education programmes for youth need to be given the highest priority because in most parts of the world the youth form an extremely large segment of society and their education is of the greatest importance for political, economic, social and cultural development of the society in which they live. The programmes of adult education for youth should take account not only of their learning needs, but should enable them to orient themselves for the society of the future.

VIII. THE RELATIONS BETWEEN ADULT EDUCATION AND WORK

39. Having regard to the close connexion between guaranteeing the right to education and the right to work, and to the need to promote the participation of all, whether wage-earners or not, in adult education programmes, not only by reducing the constraints to which they are subject but also by providing them

with the opportunity of using in their work the knowledge, qualifications or aptitudes which adult education programmes are designed to make available to them, and of finding in work a source of personal fulfilment and advancement, and a stimulus to creative activity in both work and social life, measures should be taken:

(a) to ensure that, in the formulation of the curriculum of adult education programmes and activities, the working experience of adults should be taken into account;

(b) to improve the organization and conditions of work and, in particular, to alleviate the arduous character of work and reduce and adjust working hours;

(c) to promote the granting of educational leave during working time, without loss of remuneration or subject to the payment of compensatory remuneration and payments for the purpose of offsetting the cost of the education received and to use any other appropriate aid to facilitate education or up-dating during working life;

(d) to protect the employment of persons thus assisted;

(e) to offer comparable facilities to housewives and other home-makers and to non-wage-earners, particularly those of limited means.

40. Member States should encourage or facilitate the inclusion in collective labour agreements of clauses bearing on adult education, and in particular clauses stipulating:

(a) the nature of the material possibilities and financial benefits extended to employees, and in particular those employed in sectors where rapid technological change is taking place or those threatened with being laid off, with a view to their participation in adult education programmes;

(b) the manner in which technical or professional qualifications acquired through adult education are taken into account in determining the employment category and in establishing the level of remuneration.

41. Member States should also invite employers:

(a) to anticipate and publicize, by level and type of qualification, their skilled manpower requirements and the methods of recruitment which are envisaged to meet such needs;

(b) to organize or develop a recruitment system such as will encourage their employees to seek to improve their occupational qualifications.

42. In connexion with adult training programmes organized by employers for their staff, Member States should encourage them to ensure that:

(a) employees participate in the preparation of the programmes;

(b) those taking part in such programmes are chosen in consultation with the workers' representative bodies;

(c) participants receive a certificate of training or paper qualification on completion of the programme enabling them to satisfy third parties that they have completed a given course or received a given qualification.

43. Measures should be taken with a view to promoting the participation of adults belonging to labouring, agricultural or craft communities in the implementation of adult education programmes intended for such communities; to this end they should be granted special facilities with the aim of enabling the workers to take those decisions which primarily concern them.

IX. MANAGEMENT, ADMINISTRATION, CO-ORDINATION AND FINANCING OF ADULT EDUCATION

44. There should be set up, at all levels, international, regional

national and local:

(a) structures or procedures for consultation and co-ordination between public authorities which are competent in the field of adult education;

(b) structures or procedures for consultation, co-ordination and harmonization between the said public authorities, the representatives of adult learners and the entire range of bodies carrying out adult education programmes or activities designed to promote the development of such programmes.

It should be among the principal functions of these structures, for which resources should be made available, to identify the objectives, to study the obstacles encountered, to propose and, where appropriate, carry out the measures necessary for implementation of the adult education policy and to evaluate the progress made.

45.   There should be set up at national level, and, where appropriate, at sub-national level, structures for joint action and co-operation between the public authorities and bodies responsible for adult education on the one hand and the public or private bodies responsible for radio and television on the other.

It should be among the principal functions of these structures to study, propose and, where appropriate, carry out measures designed to:

(a) ensure that the mass media make a substantial contribution to leisure-time occupations and to the education of the people;

(b) guarantee freedom of expression, through the mass media, for all opinions and trends in the field of adult education;

(c) promote the cultural or scientific value and the educational qualities of programmes as a whole;

(d) establish a two-way flow of exchanges between those responsible for or those professionally engaged in educational programmes broadcast by radio or television and the persons for whom the programmes are intended.

46. Member States should ensure that the public authorities, while assuming their own specific responsibilities for the development of adult education;

(a) encourage, by laying down an appropriate legal and financial framework, the creation and development of adult education associations and consortia on a voluntary and administratively independent basis;

(b) provide non-governmental bodies participating in adult education programmes, or in action designed to promote such programmes, with technical or financial resources enabling them to carry out their task;

(c) see that such non-governmental bodies enjoy the freedom of opinion and the technical and educational autonomy which are necessary in order to give effect to the principles set forth in paragraph 2 above;

(d) take appropriate measures to ensure the educational and technical efficiency and quality of programmes or action conducted by bodies in receipt of contributions from public funds.

47. The proportion of public funds, and particularly of public funds earmarked for education, allocated to adult education, should match the importance of such education for social, cultural and economic development, as recognized by each Member State within the framework of this Recommendation. The total allocation of funds to adult education should cover at least:

(a) provision of suitable facilities or adaptation of existing facilities;

(b) production of all kinds of learning materials;

(c) remuneration and further training of educators;

(d) research and information expenses;

(e) compensation for loss of earnings;

(f) tuition, and, where necessary and if possible, accommodation and travel costs of trainees.

48. Arrangements should be made to ensure, on a regular basis, the necessary funds for adult education programmes and action designed to promote the development of such programmes; it should be recognized that the public authorities, including local authorities, credit organizations, provident societies and national insurance agencies where they exist, and employers should contribute to these funds to an extent commensurate with their respective responsibilities and resources.

49 The necessary measures should be taken to obtain optimum use of resources made available for adult education. All available resources, both material and human, should be mobilized to this end.

50. For the individual, lack of funds should not be an obstacle to participation in adult education programmes. Member States should ensure that financial assistance for study purposes is available for those who need it to undertake adult education. The participation of members of underprivileged social groups should, as a general rule, be free of charge.

X.   INTERNATIONAL CO-OPERATION

51. Member States should strengthen their co-operation, whether on a bilateral or multilateral basis, with a view to promoting the development of adult education, the improvement of its content and methods, and efforts to find new educational strategies.

To this end, they should endeavour to incorporate specific clauses bearing on adult education in international agreements concerned with co-operation in the fields of education, science and culture, and to promote the development and strengthening of a special division for adult education in Unesco.

52. Member States should put their experience with regard to adult education at the disposal of other Member States by providing them with technical assistance and, in appropriate cases, with material or financial assistance.

They should systematically support adult education activities conducted in countries so wishing, through Unesco and through other international organizations, including non-governmental organizations, with a view to social, cultural and economic development in the countries concerned.

Care should be taken to ensure that international co-operation does not take the form of a mere transfer of structures, curricula, methods and techniques which have originated elsewhere, but consists rather in prompting and stimulating development within the countries concerned, through the establishment of appropriate institutions and well co-ordinated structures adapted to the particular circumstances of those countries.

53. Measures should be taken at national, regional and international level:

(a) with a view to making regular exchanges of information and documentation on the strategies, structures, contents, methods and results of adult education and on relevant research;

(b) with a view to training educators capable of working away from their home country, particularly under bilateral or multilateral technical assistance programmes.

These exchanges should be made on a systematic basis, particularly between countries facing the same problems and so placed as to be capable of applying the same solutions; to this end, meetings should be organized, more especially on a regional or sub-regional basis, with a view to publicizing relevant experiments and studying to what extent they are reproducible; similarly, joint machinery should be set up in order to ensure a better return on the research which is undertaken.

Member States should foster agreements on the preparation and adoption of international standards in important fields, such as the teaching of foreign languages and basic studies, with a view to helping create a universally accepted unit-credit system.

54. Measures should be taken with a view to the optimum dissemination and utilization of audio-visual equipment and materials, as well as educational programmes and the material objects in which they are embodied. In particular, it would be appropriate:

(a) to adapt such dissemination and utilization to the various countries' social needs and conditions, bearing in mind their specific cultural characteristics and level of development;

(b) to remove, as far as possible, the obstacles to such dissemination and utilization resulting from the regulations governing commercial or intellectual property.

55. In order to facilitate international co-operation, Member States should apply to adult education the standards recommended at international level, in particular with regard to the presentation of statistical data.

56. Member States should support the action undertaken by Unesco, as the United Nations Specialized Agency competent in this field, in its efforts to develop adult education, particularly in the fields of training, research and evaluation.

57. Member States should regard adult education as a matter of global and universal concern, and should deal with the practical consequences which arise therefrom, furthering the establishment of a new international order, to which Unesco, as an expression of the world community in educational, scientific and cultural matters, is committed.

Appendix C

Resolutions passed at a seminar on "Structures of Adult Education in Developing Countries, with special reference to Africa" sponsored by Unesco and the African Adult Education Association.[1]

Recommendation 1

In order to make manifest the significance of adult education in national development, governments should consider formulating goals for adult education which outline not only national objectives, but which also take account of the views and needs of communities and individuals.

Recommendation 2

That planning units on education and economic and social development should include adult educationists.

Recommendation 3

That care be taken to ensure that the content of adult education bears a close relationship to the stated goals, giving proper consideration to both national and individual needs.

Recommendation 4

That adult education specialists be included in the staffs of national curriculum development centres.

Recommendation 5

A close working relationship should be established between the statutory and non-statutory agencies so that all the resources available can be used in a co-ordinated and co-operative manner to the greatest benefit of the community as a whole.

Recommendation 6

That effective administrative structures should be established for

[1]Taken from the Final Report of the Seminar on *Structures for Adult Education in Developing Countries, with special reference to Africa,* Unesco, Paris, 1975.

adult education, extending from the national to local levels.

Recommendation 7
That appropriate legislation should be enacted to ensure that adult education is placed on a firm legal basis, on an equal footing with the other branches of education.

Recommendation 8
That some formula be devised to ensure that adult education is soundly financed. This might necessitate allocating a fixed percentage of the gross educational budget.

Recommendation 9
That a relationship of mutual assistance should be fostered between the formal system of education and adult education.

Recommendation 10
That Member States should develop regular statistical surveys of adult education activities along the lines proposed in the *Unesco "Manual" for the Collection of Adult Education Statistics.*

Recommendation 11
Since people are the foundation on which all educational structures ultimately rest, the provision of adequate training facilities for adult educationists should be regarded as a first priority.

Recommendation 12
That governments be requested to establish a structure for research in adult education, linked appropriately with universities, departments and agencies concerned with adult education and effectively staffed and financed.

Recommendation 13
Evaluation should be an integral part of all adult education activities, and to this end, adequate arrangements should be made for the preparation of specialists in this field.

Recommendation 14
That the methods adopted for adult education should be reviewed to ensure that the most effective service is being offered to adult learners. This review should take account of the need for an adequate supply of materials of various forms which are required for adult education.

Recommendation 15

Consideration should be given in every country to the establishment of a central clearing system for all forms of information on adult education.

Recommendation 16

That comprehensive inventories of physical facilities should be maintained, and that all public educational premises should be available for adult educational activities, when not being used for their primary purpose.

Recommendation 17

That due attention should be paid by governments and others engaged in adult education to strengthen and maintain links with organizations of a regional and international character concerned with adult education.

APPENDIX D

Ministry of National Education
Organization Structure, Tanzania

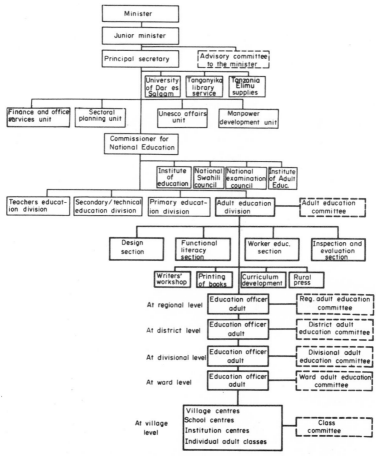

Taken from the Final Report of the Seminar on "Structures for Adult
Education in Developing Countries, with special referece to Africa",
Unesco, 1975.

189

Proposal to form an Adult Education Council in Swaziland, made to the Government by the National Education Commission, 1975[1]

Establishment of the Adult Education Council

10. (1) An Adult Education Council is hereby established composed of the following members—

(a) the Chief Education Officer (or in his absence his deputy) who shall be Chairman;

(b) one nominee of the Ministry of Agriculture;

(c) one nominee of the Sabenta Society;

(d) one nominee of the National Education Board;

(e) one nominee of the Ministry of Finance and Economic Planning;

(f) one nominee of the Department of Establishments and Training;

(g) one nominee of the Ministry of Local Administration;

(h) one nominee of the Ministry of Health;

(i) one member appointed by the Swazi National Council;

(j) one nominee of the Ministry of Education who shall be secretary;

(k) one representative of the National Board for Higher Education;

(l) one nominee of the Swaziland Conference of Churches;

(m) one nominee from the Swaziland National Association of Teachers;

---

[1]*Report of the National Education Commission, 1975*, Swaziland Government, 1975, pp. 71-73.

(n) one nominee from the University of Botswana, Lesotho and Swaziland (Swaziland),

(o) one nominee from the Ministry of Commerce and Co-operatives;

(p) one nominee of the Federation of Employers.

(2) The members referred to in Section 10(1) shall hold office for a period of three years but shall be eligible for re-appointment at the end of their term of office.

Functions of the Council

11. (1) The Minister may refer to the Adult Education Council for its advice in any matter relating to adult education.

(2) The Adult Education Council shall, when any matter is referred to it under subsection (1), consider such matter and submit to the Minister its advice thereon.

(3) The Adult Education Council may submit to the Minister its advice on any matter relating to adult education.

(4) The Adult Education Council shall advise the Minister on the following:

(1) establishment of adult schools and classes—no person, or group of persons, shall establish an adult school, or add classes to an existing school, without having received the recommendation writing of the Council which may give its recommendation thereto on being satisfied as to the agreement of the owner of the land on which it is proposed to establish the school or add classes, the qualification of the teachers whom it is proposed to employ, the nature of the subjects to be taught, and the provision to be made for the general conduct and discipline of the adult school or classes:

provided that the Council may refuse any application for approval of the establishment of a school or classes if it is satisfied that—

(a) the number of potential adults in the area capable of

benefiting from the facilities offered by the proposed school is too small to warrant the establishment of such school; or

(b) the proposed site or premises is unsuitable or inadequate for the type of school sought to be established; or

(c) the proposed school will not be in the best interest of education in relation to the best use of Government funds, or otherwise; or

(d) adequate provision already exists for the type of education which it is proposed to give in the school.

(2) Where the Council has refused its approval under the provisions of subsection (1) and subsection (2) of section 4 hereof the applicant for such approval may, within thirty days of the date of such refusal, appeal to the Minister, whose decision shall be final, but the Minister should give his reasons to the National Education Board.

(3) To recommend to the Minister the way in which grants shall be distributed for adult education and also to determine the situation of such schools.

(4) To advise on payment to communities and other agencies by Government which ordinarily, shall be half the capital costs involved in any authorised undertaking.

(5) To advise on general standards that have to be achieved by the adult education centres.

(6) To keep in review the need for teachers in the adult education centres and to such end to coordinate its activities with those of the National Education Board.

(7) To keep in review and make recommendations to the Minister regarding the salary structure of all teachers in the adult education centres.

(8) To submit to the Minister for his approval plans for the promotion and development of adult education.

(9) To exercise such other functions as may be conferred upon

it by this Order or any other law.

(10) Subject to the directions of the Minister, to do all such acts and things as may be necessary or expedient for the efficient discharge of its functions.

(11) The Council shall be subject to the financial regulations of the Government currently in force.

(12) The Council shall meet on not less than one occasion in each quarter of the year and at a time and place to be fixed by the Chairman.

A Small Basic Collection of Books in the English Language on Adult and Non-formal Education in Developing Countries

1. An international perspective on education:
   Learning to be, being the Report of the International Commission on Education, Unesco, Paris, 1973.

2. An international survey of adult education:
   The Education of Adults: a World Perspective, by John Lowe (Unesco/OISE, 1975).

3. Theory and practice of adult education in developing countries:
   Adult Education in Developing Countries, by Edwin K. Townsend Coles (Pergamon Press, 1977).

4. Basic handbook for administrators:
   Adult Education Handbook, edited by the Institute of Adult Education of the University of Dar-es-Salaam (Tanzania Publishing House, 1973).

5. Adult learning:
   How Adults Learn, by J. R. Kidd (Association Press, 1974).

6. Adult teaching:
   Teaching Adults; a Handbook for Developing Countries, by R. Prosser and R. Clarke (East African Literature Bureau, 1972).

7. Programmes for rural populations:
   Attacking Rural Poverty, by P. H. Coombs and M. Ahmed (Johns Hopkins University Press, 1974).

8. Literacy:
   Practical Guide to Functional Literacy, a Method of Training

for Development and *The Training of Functional Literacy Personnel, a Practical Guide* (both published by Unesco, 1973).

9. Health education:
    Health by the People (World Health Organization, 1975).

10. Audio-visual aids:
    Aids to Teaching and Learning, by Helen Coppen (Pergamon Press, 1968).

11. Correspondence education:
    Teaching by correspondence, by Rene Erdos (Unesco/Longmans, 1967).

12. Community development:
    Training for Community Development, by T. R. Batten (Oxford University Press, 1969).

13. Library services:
    The Organization of Small Libraries, by Joan Allen (Oxford University Press, 1961).

Index